The Truth About Oscar Slater
[With the Prisoner's Own Story]

William Park

1926 1927

The Making of Modern Law collection of legal archives constitutes a genuine revolution in historical legal research because it opens up a wealth of rare and previously inaccessible sources in legal, constitutional, administrative, political, cultural, intellectual, and social history. This unique collection consists of three extensive archives that provide insight into more than 300 years of American and British history. These collections include:

Legal Treatises, 1800-1926: over 20,000 legal treatises provide a comprehensive collection in legal history, business and economics, politics and government.

Trials, 1600-1926: nearly 10,000 titles reveal the drama of famous, infamous, and obscure courtroom cases in America and the British Empire across three centuries.

Primary Sources, 1620-1926: includes reports, statutes and regulations in American history, including early state codes, municipal ordinances, constitutional conventions and compilations, and law dictionaries.

These archives provide a unique research tool for tracking the development of our modern legal system and how it has affected our culture, government, business – nearly every aspect of our everyday life. For the first time, these high-quality digital scans of original works are available via print-on-demand, making them readily accessible to libraries, students, independent scholars, and readers of all ages.

The BiblioLife Network

This project was made possible in part by the BiblioLife Network (BLN), a project aimed at addressing some of the huge challenges facing book preservationists around the world. The BLN includes libraries, library networks, archives, subject matter experts, online communities and library service providers. We believe every book ever published should be available as a high-quality print reproduction; printed on-demand anywhere in the world. This insures the ongoing accessibility of the content and helps generate sustainable revenue for the libraries and organizations that work to preserve these important materials.

The following book is in the "public domain" and represents an authentic reproduction of the text as printed by the original publisher. While we have attempted to accurately maintain the integrity of the original work, there are sometimes problems with the original work or the micro-film from which the books were digitized. This can result in minor errors in reproduction. Possible imperfections include missing and blurred pages, poor pictures, markings and other reproduction issues beyond our control. Because this work is culturally important, we have made it available as part of our commitment to protecting, preserving, and promoting the world's literature.

GUIDE TO FOLD-OUTS MAPS and OVERSIZED IMAGES

The book you are reading was digitized from microfilm captured over the past thirty to forty years. Years after the creation of the original microfilm, the book was converted to digital files and made available in an online database.

In an online database, page images do not need to conform to the size restrictions found in a printed book. When converting these images back into a printed bound book, the page sizes are standardized in ways that maintain the detail of the original. For large images, such as fold-out maps, the original page image is split into two or more pages

Guidelines used to determine how to split the page image follows:

• Some images are split vertically; large images require vertical and horizontal splits.
• For horizontal splits, the content is split left to right.
• For vertical splits, the content is split from top to bottom.
• For both vertical and horizontal splits, the image is processed from top left to bottom right.

THE LATE LIEUT JOHN T TRENCH
From a photograph taken while an officer of the Glasgow
Criminal Investigation Department

THE TRUTH ABOUT
OSCAR SLATER

[With the Prisoner's Own Story]

By

WILLIAM PARK

WITH A STATEMENT BY
SIR ARTHUR CONAN DOYLE

———

o

THE PSYCHIC PRESS
2, VICTORIA STREET
LONDON, S W

A

DEDICATED

TO THE

MEMORY OF THE

Late Lieut. John T. Trench,
King's Medallist, Glasgow,

who, as a public officer of the police force, actuated by an inspiring sense of justice, sacrificed his career and pension in a personal attempt to rescue from a life's detention in prison, and with a desire to save others from the risk of a similar cruel fate, a man whom he believed on his conscience to have been wrongfully convicted in the Scottish High Court of Justiciary, and for which noble act he was dismissed and ruined.

INTRODUCTION TO THE CASE

By ARTHUR CONAN DOYLE, M.D , LL D

It is certain that the case of the alien German Jew, who bore the pseudonym of Oscar Slater, will live in the history of criminology as a miscarriage of justice of a character very unusual in the records of our Courts There have been others, which have been more immediately serious in their results, for innocent men have lost their lives on the scaffold , but such cases, however deplorable, could be excused on the grounds that the circumstantial evidence appeared to be so strong that the mistake could be condoned) But in this case, the error is manifest It has been pointed out again and again and each successive Scottish Secretary has been appealed to without result None of them, apparently, has ever gone into the case for himself, which is essential in order that a really independent mind may be brought to

5

This, of course, is what ACD did.

bear upon it As a result, in spite of the fact that there is not one point of the evidence which does not crumble to pieces when it is touched, this unfortunate man, after eighteen years, is still eating out his heart in Peterhead Jail

Shortly after his conviction I published a little book to show this man's innocence, and I brought out a further version of it in 1914, when a Single Commissioner was appointed to examine the matter, and there was some hope that justice would be done. The functions of the Commission, however, were so limited by the terms of its appointment, that matters of vital moment to a genuine inquiry—including the conduct of the police in the preparation of the case—were excluded from investigation

After that I despaired of any good result, and it is possible that I might never have touched the matter again, had it not been for the writer of this book. He is a Glasgow journalist with vast experience in important criminal trials His record in this matter has been splendid. From the beginning he had the logical mind, which showed him clearly the weakness of the case, and also the abstract sense of justice, which would never allow his soul to be at rest while a patent wrong was being

1912

1914

done to a helpless and friendless man. During all these years, we have been in touch over the matter, and I have always been stimulated by his tenacity of purpose. He has been a sleuth-hound, in following the trail, and a bull-dog in keeping his grip. Gradually the evidence in favour of Slater became more and more over-powering and, now that it is set forth in sequence, I do not think that any reasonable human being could fail to be convinced of this man's complete innocence and of the very unsatisfactory procedure adopted which led to his erroneous conviction.

The genesis of the error is clear enough. It was supposed, though it has never been proved, that a diamond brooch had been taken from Miss Gilchrist's room at the time of the murder. Following this, the police discovered that Slater had left Glasgow for America and that he had pawned a diamond brooch. With very undue haste they appear to have jumped to the conclusion that this brooch was the supposed missing brooch of Miss Gilchrist, and that Slater must have committed the murder. The pawned brooch, however, was one which belonged to Slater, and the police became aware of this fact (as the writer shows) before Slater sailed for

America Slater, moreover, had been extremely open about his movements, he had made his preparations for going to America with the greatest deliberation, and carried them out in the same leisurely and open manner after the date when the crime was committed as he had done previously The result is, that at the date when Slater sailed, the pawned brooch having been shown to be his own property, *there appears to have been no evidence to connect him with the crime.* Such being the case, how is it that a cable was sent to New York to have him arrested on arrival? It seems impossible to avoid the conclusion that the cable was a grave official blunder against Slater.

Each clue against Slater crumbles to pieces when examined There was the brooch. We have seen what that was worth. Then came the idea that he had fled from Glasgow. This played a great part in the trial, though by that time any impartial inquirer would have been well aware that the departure had been arranged long before and that Slater had entered his own name in the register of the Liverpool Hotel —a thing inconceivable in the case of a man who had reason to fear pursuit. That clue is gone. Then there is the question of motive.

There was no possible motive (The object of the assassin seems to have been papers, since he opened a box which contained papers and left untouched objects of value, which were under his nose) No link was ever traced between Slater, a stranger in the City, and this retired Scottish lady (What could he possibly want her papers for?) The idea is ridiculous Then there is the weapon A small hammer from a half-crown card was found in Slater's trunk (No stains of blood were shown upon it, nor on any of his clothes) Yet this was put down as the weapon with which those frightful injuries had been inflicted Blunder follows blunder—each more absurd than the last and all to be clearly followed in Mr Park's inquisition Last of all comes the alleged identification, which, as Mr. Park shows, was of the weakest possible description These are the shreds and patches out of which the prosecution was built

Since the trial a fresh witness has come along, whose testimony would not only exonerate Slater, but would seem to be the starting point for a real investigation, though the scent has gone very cold in the course of the years This woman, as will be seen in Mr Park's pages, was run into and actually knocked down by the

* Once correct premise is adopted, Slater's motive falls apart.

man in his flight (This runaway, the witness states, in no way resembled Slater, but presented sufficient peculiarities of dress to make him a marked man.

Who is to blame for this great and persistent miscarriage of justice? There were many, in greater or lesser degree. Judge Guthrie is to blame, because he did not bring out the points which would have thrown a light on the truth, and because he showed an unconscious bias against the prisoner. The Lord Advocate is to blame, because his speech was a heated and unmeasured one, containing statements which were errors in fact and yet which were passed by the judge and were calculated to affect deeply the mind of the jury. The witnesses were to blame, who allowed their testimony to vary at different times and stages of the proceedings. Each successive Secretary of State for Scotland is to blame, because he did not use his own independent mind to find out an obvious truth. Sheriff Millar is to blame for the conduct of the white-washing committee of 1914, but, above all, the Procurator Fiscal and the police, who had the conduct of the case, are those who bear the heaviest load.

There are one or two bright spots in the

general darkness. One is the unceasing efforts and the unselfish work of the writer of this book Another is the honest work of the police lawyer, Cook, who never bowed his knee to Baal and suffered in consequence.) But most outstanding of all was the heroic detective, Trench, who ruined his career in defence of right. Trench is more like one of Charles Reade's wonderful heroes, than a man of this workaday world.) He held the King's medal, and was one of the trusty band told off to guard Royalty on its visits to Scotland He rose to distinction in the Glasgow police force, and gained such a reputation that he was borrowed by other towns when difficult cases arose. From the first, he seems to have been on the right line in the Slater case, but was unable to influence the activities of his official superiors. His conscience was clearly not at rest and, finally, he felt constrained to risk his whole career and his pension in an effort to get his views before the public In order to do so, it would be necessary for him to reveal matters learned by him in the course of his professional duties, and this was against the local laws of the police force, however much it might be in the interests of public justice. Knowing this, Trench asked for an indemnity from the Scottish Office against the probable anger of his superiors, and it was with the assurance that he had obtained this indemnity that he bore witness. The sequel, however, shocking to relate, was that he was immediately afterwards turned out of the force and deprived of his pension on the very charge which he had foreseen and, as he thought, provided against.

There was worse to come, however, and the Trench case provides a scandal only second to that out of which it arose. Trench and Cook, the lawyer who had acted with him, were presently arrested upon a criminal charge, which was so absurd that the judge at once laughed it out of court. Cook, however, took the matter greatly to heart, and it is said to have contributed to his death a short time afterwards. Trench did some good service in connection with the War, and, before the outbreak, was instrumental in securing the arrest of Dr. Karl Graves, a most important foreign spy, who had designs on the Forth Bridge. He was, however, a stricken man from the time of his disgrace, and he sank into a decline from which he never rallied. It is certainly a most remarkable fact that, in 1909, Slater should have been within twenty-four hours of being hanged and that he should now be alive, while Guthrie the judge, Hart the Procurator Fiscal, Lambie, the chief witness, Millar, the Chairman of the Committee, Trench and Cook, the two men, who stood out for justice, and several other protagonists have passed away

A word should be said, even at the risk of digression, of Trench's work on the Dundee case, which closely succeeded that of Slater, and which bears a curious resemblance to it A murder had been committed, and was attributed to a wandering American Bohemian named Warner. The man was arrested at Maidstone and a dozen identifications were secured, one witness bursting into tears and declaring "I know that I am putting the rope round his neck, but that's the man" Trench, however, went more deeply into the case, and he showed clearly by a visit to Antwerp that the prisoner had pawned his waistcoat there at the very time when he should have been at Dundee Trench's work on this Slater case was equally just and intelligent, but for it he was ruined, and this after obtaining, as he imagined, full leave to speak the truth

From time to time one hears some word of poor Slater from behind his prison walls like the wail of some wayfarer who has fallen into a pit and implores aid from the passers-by A life sentence is usually remitted at the end of fifteen years, but his martyrdom has now lasted for nearly twenty   I have no doubt that, maddened by the injustice and by the sense of his lost life and the passing years, he has occasionally been driven into some wild protest which has been counted against him   I wonder which of us would have more self-restraint. It is notable that I have been in touch with several of his fellow convicts who have come out, and that they are agreed that his innocence is recognised by his criminal companions, and there could be no more knowing jury than that Once he managed to smuggle out to me a despairing cry for help in a glazed paper concealed in a comrade's mouth) I could, alas ! do no more than I had already done. I did, however, on the strength of it, send another appeal to the present Secretary of Scotland, and received the usual official note in reply) Verily, some of these gentlemen will have a bill to pay one day. There is no happiness possible in the Beyond until one has obtained the complete forgiveness of each person one has wronged

Finally, we may ask, what can now be done ?

I fear very little can be done for Slater Who
can restore the vanished years ? But his name
may be cleared, and possibly some small provision
made for his declining years He is fifty-eight,
so he would find it hard to take up life anew
But above all, for the credit of British justice,
for the discipline of the police force, and for
the teaching of officials that their duty to the
public has to be done, *a thorough public inquiry
should be made into the whole matter But let it
be a real enquiry*, with impartial men who are
resolute for truth and justice upon the Bench
Only when this has been done will the public
mind be at ease

The case has a very much wider application
than at first sight appears It gives an opportunity of going behind the scenes Important
evidence in Slater's favour appears not to have
been called attention to , and this neglect calls
for thorough and careful investigation and
explanation

As shown in the narrative, among several
supposed witnesses favourable to Slater, there
was one whose evidence would have completely
upset the theory of the police, and yet he was
discarded altogether I allude to the man,
McBrayne The Institution of the Court of

Criminal Appeal does not meet the case at all, so that this is an English as well as a Scottish problem. Such an appeal is connected only with things said or done at the trial, and yet in this Slater case, and possibly in many others the Judge is as badly informed as the Jury or the Public as to the true facts Our police force and our judiciary are probably at present the best in the world, but there is a rotten patch here which needs probing and cutting out It is not merely Slater's innocence—important as this is to the individual—but the protection of prisoners in general, which is the aim of this work If this could be accomplished, then the martyrdom of this one man might seem to have had some sort of object and result.

What is needed is the revision of our criminal system by the appointment of some higher authority to inspect and examine the internal work of the police in England and of Fiscals in Scotland in the preparation of a case In this case, Lambie, an essential witness, deposed in New York, quite early in the proceedings, that her deposition was written and rewritten so many times she could not count them. " More than I could tell you," she said. The truth does not need such editing as that.

It is to be hoped that such Higher Authority as is indicated might recommend that Head Constables and Fiscals in preparing a case *should be obliged by stringent law, to acquaint the prisoner's friends with any evidence which they come across in the prisoner's favour* This man, McBrayne, for example, was in touch with the police, but the Defence do not seem to have been aware of his existence Again, it should be a dire offence for the police or their solicitor to keep back, carelessly or otherwise, anything material from the court. It is simply inconceivable that an honourable gentleman like the Lord Advocate would have permitted himself to make the statements he did, had he been properly instructed as to all the real facts in possession of the police It is no answer to this to say that it is the duty of the Defence to find out and to expound their side of the case The police have the investigations in their own hands, and they have an inside knowledge which the defence cannot reach. The police can put up the best legal talent to state their case, while the prisoner, if he be a poor man, has to take what he can get. If, negligently or otherwise, material facts are kept back, a prisoner may be a convicted man before he enters the dock Let the Chief Constable or the Fiscal be personally responsible for any miscarriage of justice through the non-disclosure (however unintentional) of material facts in a prisoner's favour.

A writer in the eighteenth century has said . " The Law Courts perpetually need reminding that they are not above the public , the public is above them " The reminder is as needful in the twentieth century as in the eighteenth In the " law courts " we must include the whole machinery of justice. The revelations of the Slater case show that if circumstances should seem to be against them, no man or woman is safe. By a curious chance, even as I write these words, Judge Avory, from the bench, has said : " The evidence is unsatisfactory because witnesses have been shown photographs before identification " If Judge Guthrie had taken the same view, where would the Slater prosecution have been ? It is indeed a lamentable story of official blundering from start to finish. But eighteen years have passed and an innocent man still wears the convict's dress.

ARTHUR CONAN DOYLE.

The Truth about Oscar Slater

The Tragedy and its Discovery

On Monday, 21st December, 1908, an aged, unmarried lady, named Marion Gilchrist, who was in occupation of a seven-roomed flat at 15 Queen's Terrace, West Princes Street, Glasgow, was done to death with dramatic daring and swiftness and with ruthless exhibitions of brutality. The murder occurred at an hour in the early evening when the streets in that populous area were busiest with the movements of pedestrians, and the residents in the adjoining flats most keenly susceptible to alarm, so that a lonely occupant, such as the unfortunate victim happened momentarily to be when she was struck down, might have dreamed herself, immune from intrusion and attack. In the same set of flats immediately beneath the dining-room where she was engaged in leisurely reading a magazine, at the hour when the assailant entered, there were seated in after-tea domestic ease a Mr and Miss Adams. A few minutes earlier they had been joined by a third member of the family, a Mrs Liddell. This lady, as she approached the residence of her brother, had observed leaning over a railing in front of Miss Gilchrist's dwelling, a man to whose presence she then attached no suspicions Afterwards, she came to consider him as possibly the assailant who had stationed himself there in vigilant wait for the appearance on the street of the servant maid from the flat upstairs. This might be to him the signal that the coast was clear for his entrance and only the aged and defenceless lady to be dealt with single-handed The maid each evening left the residence of Miss Gilchrist punctually at this seven o'clock hour to fetch her mistress a newspaper, upon which errand she was detained never more than ten minutes. It was this brief interval, when the old lady would be left by herself, which the assailant snatched as his opportunity to enter and accomplish his terrible mission

The presence within earshot of the Adams people, immediately beneath his victim, and the inevitable certainty of the maid's reappearance within ten minutes, bespoke an almost reckless disregard for his own safety on the part of the assailant , though this had already been shown in his selecting that inopportune seven o'clock hour for the perpetration of a deed in which all

restraint in the employment of violence was
to be thrown to the winds. Mrs Liddell was
scarcely seated in the flat below when the first
of the savage blows rained upon the head of
the victim, as it lay in contact with the floor,
followed by others in rapid succession, was
heard by the three members of the Adams
family with startled and arrested attention

Pausing to consider what might be the cause
of such unusual and violent noises from over-
head, they judged something seriously amiss
to be happening in the flat of their neighbour
which, as friends, they could not permit to
pass unheeded. Miss Adams, moreover, had
long been under a promise to Miss Gilchrist that,
in the event of alarm, which would be signalled
to them by three knocks on the floor, the Adams
would go to her assistance. It was decided
accordingly that the cause of the disturbances
should be investigated without a moment's
delay The brother thereupon rushed upstairs
to the door of Miss Gilchrist's flat to ascertain
the cause of the uproar. Failing to obtain
admission, he paused in wonder at the doorstep Peering through the side glass panels to
ascertain if there were any movement, only a
light was to be seen in the hall. He then
vigorously pulled the bell. To this urgent summons there was no response. A minute later

there came a recurrence of the ominous noises
from within, which he interpreted as being
possibly caused by the maid servant in the act
of breaking sticks   The assailant within, hearing
this tugging at the bell—"rude pulls," Mr Adams
said they were—could scarcely have failed to
realise that his indiscreet violence had roused
and brought to the door some alarmed and
enquiring resident or even attracted some
passer-by from the street, for the outer door had
been left ajar on his entering the stairway
which led up to the house. This was an interruption which signified that he might find his
escape obstructed and his own neck in danger
Yet that dread did not deter him or slacken
the rain of his blows. Renewed sounds, like
" the chopping of firewood," were heard by
the eager listener at the door. Considering these
still to be the work of the maid, who was refusing
him admission, Mr. Adams, his mind now
somewhat eased of its suspicions, retraced his
steps downstairs to report to his sisters. By
this time the ladies, far from having had their
apprehensions quieted, were still more upset
by hearing further heavy noises, so violent they
thought their ceiling " like to crack "; and,
dissatisfied with their brother's explanations
of his abortive visit, bade him hasten upstairs
once more. Here, having again pulled the

bell and waited at the door, impotent as before
to do or ascertain anything, he was joined by
the servant-maid, Helen Lambie by name,
returning from her errand with the newspaper
Mr Adams lost no time in acquainting her
with the occasion of his unexpected presence
and his alarm as to what was going on inside
Without betrayal of concern, the servant produced her keys and found the two locks, one a
patent lock and the other a Chubb, untampered
with, just as she had left them   Opening the
door, she stepped into the hall.   Mr Adams, in
expectant mood, remained stationed at the
doorstep   Presently, the suspicious sounds
having entirely ceased, a man was seen to emerge
quietly from a bedroom where a light was
visible which had not been burning when
the servant left the house ten minutes earlier
Affecting a courteous and pleasant smile,
intended to disarm suspicion, the man, who was
of most gentlemanly appearance, glided softly
through the hall to the door, and having gained
its open exit, at once dashed madly downstairs
—" like greased lightning," as Mr Adams
graphically described it—and was heard to
bang the outer street door furiously behind him.
Following some useless talk from the maid,
offering explanations, without investigation of
the possible cause of the noises, Mr Adams

recalled her to a more befitting sense of the responsible situation in which they stood   He begged her to see to her mistress.   First visiting the kitchen, and then the bedroom, in each case without result, the maid entered the dining-room and there the crime was revealed   The screams of the servant brought Mr Adams to the scene where Miss Gilchrist was found to be lying motionless on the floor near the fireplace with a skin rug thrown over her

Removal of the covering disclosed the shocking character of the deed.   The head had been severely battered, both eyes smashed in, and there were horrid gashes and cavities on the sides of the head, with other awful injuries to the face.   The victim still breathed, but was beyond all utterance, and in a few minutes life was extinct

Near the spot where the body lay there were many evidences of the ruthless ferocity of the attack   The adjacent articles, including the edge of the table-cover, were copiously splashed with blood and small pieces of displaced bone and brain-tissue were scattered round   As high as the mantelshelf above the fireplace the spurts of blood had left their traces in bespatterings on the wall.   There were similar marks on the coalbox, which had been broken and displaced from position.   These provided unmistakable evidences, not only of the number and violence of the blows, but of the heavy nature of the weapon employed by the assailant

Meanwhile, the murderer had reached the street and vanished into that thickest of all obstacles to pursuit and identification—the peopled thorough-fares of a great city Realising his mistake in omitting to challenge the man before allowing him to pass, Mr. Adams bolted downstairs and ran along the street in a direction where he saw some people The fugitive, in the brief interval, had, however, interposed a wide gap from his pursuer and he was to be seen no more. Hearing the dash of feet downstairs, the Adams sisters left their house and rushed to the street, where they were joined by the servant, Lambie, wringing her hands wildly in despair No one at that moment was to be seen anywhere on the street by these four people—a most important point to be observed in connection with the after-statement of an eye-witness—the most important witness against the prisoner—who, at the trial of Oscar Slater, swore she was present. It had been observed by Adams and Lambie, as he evaded them in the hall, that the assailant presented, so far as they could see, neither upon himself nor his garments, signs of bloodstains—a most extra-ordinary circumstance, having regard to the area and height of the blood spots in the dining-room where the assault had taken place So far as these witnesses were concerned, standing now aimlessly on the street, there was nothing more to be done. The murderer had given them the slip under their very eyes. Realising that it was no time for vain regrets, Mr. Adams hastened to the house of a doctor near by, and then summoned the police.

Doctor Adams, as by a coincidence he was named, arrived on the scene before the victim had expired. He found her still breathing, but the end speedily came. Looking round the room for evidences of the assailant and his work, this medical practitioner had his skilled eye arrested by the peculiar appearance of a heavy and old-fashioned chair standing near the victim's body, on a leg of which he observed blood still streaming He at once proceeded to make a careful examination of the article He discovered that the left back leg was drenched with blood and the inner side of each leg had also caught some spots This struck him as most peculiar since if the mere adjacency to the victim was to be accepted as accounting for the presence of the blood spots on the chair, these should have been seen on the outside of the legs, but here they were found on the inside From substances adhering to it of brain-tissue, etc., he divined that a back leg had been in actual contact with the wounds) Some of these wounds were spindle-shaped, corresponding with the leg Then again, in the area close to the head, he observed on the carpet a comparatively small quantity of blood That circumstance led him to consider there had been some interposing body over the head obstructing the spreading of the blood there) He deduced accordingly that the chair was the instrument that had been employed to encompass the death All the circumstances considered, it was the confirmed opinion of this medical gentleman that the murder had been committed in this manner. The assailant had seized the nearest chair and with it administered a series of heavy downward thrusts, driving the back leg violently against the victim's head While using the chair in these vigorous downward thrusts, the assailant, so as to keep his victim from rising or turning, had stamped a foot forcibly on her chest) The result of this pressure of the foot had been to fracture the ribs of the chest—an injury which the doctor found also to have been inflicted.

Employment of the chair in the manner described takes us back to that peculiarity of appearance of the assailant, observed by Adams and Lambie at the moment of his stealing across the hall to make for the door. So far as they could see he was entirely free from marks of blood. How he had himself escaped even the smallest share of the ejected spurts, which had so plenteously marked their presence in the area adjacent to the position of the victim, seemed a mystery   That mystery was explained by the theory of the use of the chair as the instrument of perpetration   The seat of the chair would be interposed like a shield before the person of the assailant and would catch the spurts of blood which were ejected with each thrust of the back leg in those downward smashing blows. The bottom and inside of the legs of the chair would receive the blood which would otherwise have sprinkled itself in visible display upon his garments.   Only that portion of the spurting which escaped the intervening chair would be deposited on the surroundings. These spots were found as high as the mantelshelf— nearly the level of the assailant's head—while the chair itself literally dripped   All this explained the phenomenon seen by Lambie and Adams—that the perpetrator of so bloody a murder should show neither upon himself nor his garments any obvious signs of stain

Most of the earlier commentators on the case were led astray as regards the weapon, not having been informed of the singular facts, carefully excluded at the trial of Oscar Slater, of the dripping chair and the assailant's freedom from bloodstain. Understanding of the part played by the chair in the perpetration of the crime explains another phase of the atrocity. A murderer handling a weapon, such as a crowbar or other short-shafted instrument (say, the hammer ascribed to the prisoner), in order to get in his blows upon the head of the recumbent victim, would have been obliged to crouch into a stooping posture and have thereby inevitably received upon his garments a much larger quantity of blood than one in erect position Likewise, his blows, following a very short arc, would have been directed with accuracy of aim, and the injuries accordingly would have been restricted to the head. To knock out the eyes and smash the face, as the murderer did, was no assistance to him in the act of extinguishing life. Here, however, the assailant, standing up and swinging a heavy chair, the direction of the blow would be badly controlled. Moreover, with each downward stroke, the head of the victim, which he wanted to strike, would be obscured by the descending chair, especially if he used a back leg to strike with, and the aim accordingly become entirely blinded That precisely is what must have occurred. The murderer's badly directed blows fell upon head, eyes, side of the head and face   Finally, there was the fractured chest bones caused by the assailant standing upon the victim to keep her down

Dr. Adams, we hold, correctly interpreted the method of perpetration and likewise solved the problem of the weapon which had been employed.

It was ascertained by the police on their arrival at the scene that the assailant, after the execution of his dastardly work in the dining-room, had betaken himself to the bedroom from which Adams and Lambie had seen him emerge into the hall (There he had struck a light, applied it to the gas and left behind the spent match and the box, neither of which was found to have upon it the slightest trace of blood) The assailant had then engaged himself in a hurried examination of the victim's private papers These were contained in a jewel-box, the place of deposit of which in the bedroom he evidently well knew, and which he broke open to gain his ends The papers had been ransacked, and the carpet was strewn with documents he had fingered and rejected A diamond brooch, valued at fifty pounds, was said by the servant-maid to have disappeared, but it was an inexplicable circumstance, if indeed robbery was his object, that pre-

cisely at the spot where the assailant had stood
in the act of scrutinising the papers there lay
visible and inviting appropriation other valuable
articles of jewellery, a diamond and two other
rings, a gold bracelet, a gold watch and chain
This not unsubstantial haul of jewellery—
this strange criminal had disdained to touch !

From the entrance of the assailant until his
emergence from the house, so swift was the
execution of his several acts, not more than
a dozen minutes elapsed This circumstance
showed that the murderer in his entrance could
not have been detained at the door Its examination disclosed that there had been no forcing
of the locks—a circumstance adding yet another
element of mystery to this crime of mysteries.

It appears to have been the official view of
the police, after their search and examination of
the room, that the assailant left behind him no
weapon or implement likely to account for the
awful nature of the injuries inflicted upon the
deceased They saw no crowbar or other
instrument which a supposed burglar might be
expected to carry, and they failed to note the
condition of the chair which had arrested the
attention of Dr Adams The view was thereupon adopted that there was nothing in the
room to account for the execution of the crime
From this opinion, it is certain that some of

the lesser officers engaged in the work of investigation dissented. Superintendent Douglas, for one, was so much struck with the statements given by Mr. Adams and Lambie to the effect that the assailant had shown no signs upon hands or garments of bloodstains, that he examined the washstand, soap and towels to see whether the murderer, before leaving, had done any washing, but none was discovered, and this officer, along with others, held always that it was absolutely impossible for the murderer, using any ordinary weapon, such as a hammer, to have avoided a copious spraying with blood. His conclusion coincided with the skilled opinion of Dr Adams relative to the chair, but of these two important witnesses not another word was ever heard in connection with the crime. The reasons for this will presently emerge.

From the statements of the eye-witnesses, together with the examination of the rooms, a number of clues offered themselves for investigation These were: (1) the peculiar matchbox; (2) the nature of the private papers in the box opened by the assailant, (3) the mode of entrance by him to the house; (4) the weapon employed; and (5) the missing brooch. But let us first comprehend what the official police mind understood as the interpretation of the

crime, as the result of their examinations   At
9 40 p.m that night, or two and a half hours
subsequent to the murder, the officials who
were in charge of the case issued to the Glasgow
force a notice in which there were these statements and instructions —

"Robbery appears to have been the
object of the murderer, as a *number* of boxes
in a bedroom were opened and left lying
on the floor   A large-sized crescent brooch,
set with diamonds, large diamonds in centre
graduating towards points, is missing   The
diamonds are set in silver   No trace of the
murderer has been got   Constables will
please warn booking-clerks at railway
stations *as the murderer will have bloodstains
on his clothing.*   Also warn pawns on opening
regarding brooch and keep a sharp look-
out "

This notice, in its terms, was very official but
not very precise ' The "number" of boxes
opened happened to be one, and its contents
were papers, not jewellery   Acceptance of robbery as the motive was precipitate and failed to
meet the general features of the crime

To this statement there was added a description of the assailant, as detailed by Adams and
Lambie

Let us now examine the real clues   Clues are

finger-posts in crimes of mystery which, when
properly read, eliminate the complexities and
narrow down the trails to be followed to the
goal of detection and arrest. Clues must not be
examined independently of the general features
of the crime Here the police simply closed
their eyes to the general essence of the whole
tragedy " Boxes and blood " were all that
they saw Examine the clues as discoverable
here First, the matchbox which the assailant
had left behind was of uncommon variety and
entirely dissimilar to those in use in the house
It was the old-fashioned, and then little used,
match known as the " Runaway," with a huge
chest-like box This should have proved a
most excellent clue, doubly valuable since the
assailant might have overlooked his having left
the box behind and, accordingly, omitted to
destroy in his house or office the stock from which
he took this single box. There is no trace to be
found of the clue having been followed up with
the attention it deserved One of the officers
engaged in the work of investigation Lieutenant
Trench, who saw the importance of the point,
ascertained for himself that this type of match was
sold in Glasgow only in bulk by the larger stores,
and not in single boxes That narrowed down
the sources to be tapped for information as to
purchasers Lieutenant Trench, it may be

added, in company with a brother officer, applied this test of the " Runaway " matches to the house vacated by the prisoner Slater and the clue proved abortive there. The matchbox of the murderer was well worth spending time upon to ascertain its retailers and probable purchaser.

The second clue—the private papers in the jewel-box—obviously called for inquiries to be conducted among the relatives and friends of the deceased, not omitting the servant-girl, regarding the nature of the papers the old lady secreted in the box , and, likewise, whether any person had such an interest in any document kept there, as might, for its acquisition, tempt that person to murder

The third clue—the mode of entrance, whether by keys or by the voluntary act of the deceased —was most vital ; and at a later stage we shall deal exhaustively with this aspect of the crime Until the problem of entrance was solved there was no moving away at all from the profounder elements of mystery in the crime The same applies to the weapon, already strongly suggested by Dr Adams and Superintendent Douglas and completely ignored by the police This problem, we shall see, went hand-in-hand with the problem of entrance.

The last clue was the brooch This, which

became the first of importance in the police interpretation, was in reality only negative in character. It afforded no direct trace It came into existence only if the murderer were foolish enough to pawn or exhibit it. Having regard to the considerable quantities of jewellery that had not been touched, its removal, as Sir Arthur Conan Doyle long ago pointed out, might have been only a " blind," a ruse to mislead the police into the supposition that robbery was the motive—which bait they gorged up to the neck.

The above, in brief, represents the main points of the tragedy, the discovery and flight of the assailant ; the possible clues to be followed, and the poor work in preliminary investigation done by the police, who complicated the very difficult problems before them by going off after the brooch and a burglar, omitting altogether the profounder aspects of entrance, weapon, and the search of the private papers.

News of the dastardly outrage, so daringly executed in the heart of the city, thrilled the people of Glasgow and Scotland generally. The perpetration of a crime marked by so much daring, occurring at an hour when everyone is either abroad, or, at least, alert and active, seemed a direct challenge to the police. The hue and cry for the murderer and his theft of a diamond brooch spread so widely as eventually to embrace the greater part of the civilized world, and ended, twelve days later, in the arrest at New York of the prisoner, Oscar Slater He had been pursued across the Atlantic by a cabled message to anticipate the arrival of the *Lusitania*, on which he was known to be a passenger An added sensation to his capture was his disappearance from Glasgow four days after the murder, and almost at the very hour when the police had gone to his door to make enquiries concerning a suspected clue and to effect his arrest

Slater was formally charged with the murder of Miss Gilchrist Proceedings for his extradition to Scotland were begun at New York After several days' unsatisfactory hearings the prisoner voluntarily intimated to the Court his readiness, as an innocent man, to go back to Scotland and stand his trial there. His return to Glasgow created unusual interest The river banks, as the ship came up the Clyde, were lined with thousands of spectators, actuated by the usual blend of morbidity and curiosity The authorities, in these circumstances, deemed it advisable to take him off at Renfrew, a little to the west of Glasgow, and thence by motor cars, with considerable police escort, he reached the city and became the prisoner in Scotland—

which he still is to-day—eighteen years later
The subsequent proceedings at his trial on the
murder charge were conducted at Edinburgh in
May, 1909   These occupied four days in hearing   The verdict of the Jury was " Guilty " by
a majority of 9—6, a result that would have
given him in England a new trial   Upon hearing the verdict, as intimated by the foreman of
the Jury, Slater staggered to his feet and in
broken English, he being a foreign Jew, poured
out a pathetic appeal, declaring his innocence
and protesting against the verdict, the distressing
effect of which speech upon the Court, it was said,
had never been experienced n any previous case
on record   As a consequence, the Supreme
Court of Scotland did not apparently care to
risk a renewal in the future of an ordeal so
painful   Three weeks later an Act of Sederunt
was passed whereby a prisoner, once the verdict
is announced, may be hustled downstairs to the
cells without the interval of waiting for it to be
recorded and signed   Slater's protest against
the verdict left its mark on the judicial procedure
of Scottish Courts

Sentenced to death, the obvious weakness
of the evidence against the prisoner led to a
reconsideration of his case in higher counsels, it
being everywhere held as insufficient to warrant
the verdict, and a reprieve was granted   The

official message reached Slater in Duke Street prison, Glasgow, almost on the eve of the appointed hour for his doom He is now in Peterhead Convict Establishment serving a life-commuted sentence, and is entering the nineteenth year of his captivity His case has been frequently raised in Parliament and almost unceasingly in the Press, while Sir Arthur Conan Doyle, who wrote a pamphlet to show the inadequacy of the evidence, has made three direct appeals to successive Secretaries for Scotland It is significant, however, of the utter hopelessness of an appeal to officialdom, that in response to a communication from the Glasgow solicitor of Slater, one of the lesser Scottish members of the late Coalition Government, replied ·—

"I am far too busy to take up Slater's case It is no use asking a single question. To have any effect questions must be followed up steadily and persistently The release of Slater would not be detrimental to the professional reputation of the Lord Advocate Indeed, it would be a tribute to his skill as an Advocate (not as a judge) that he had secured the conviction of a man afterwards discovered to be innocent."*

*The original of this letter is in the possession of the writer

In the interval since the trial, the most eminent publicists have attacked the case, reviewed the evidence, and exposed its weaknesses and contradictions "We march from puzzle to puzzle and from perplexity we at no point escape," declared the late Mr Andrew Lang. Since that was said, new witnesses have been discovered, and new police documents exposed, all of which have confirmed the prisoner's plea of innocence, and further condemned the shadowy and fragmentary case against the convicted man In consequence of "inside" revelations by a Glasgow officer, disclosing the existence of evidence favourable to Slater, and an allegation by that officer to the effect that the servant-girl on the night of the murder had named another man as the author of the crime, an investigation was ordered in the year 1914 The alleged inquiry was strangled at its very inception by an official instruction which ordered the Commissioner to exclude from the scope of his investigations all matters relating to the conduct of the trial The rooted impression now is that officialdom, afraid to have the scandals of the case revealed to the public, has decreed that the prisoner, who had long since passed the fifteenth year of his incarceration (a period generally recognised as the termination of a life-commuted sentence) shall die in a convict establish-

*That this did not happen ...

ment, and that in a prison grave the appeal for justice this wretched man has unceasingly and insistently made during these long years shall eventually be stifled.

The writer makes this brief excuse for another contribution to the notorious case—that he has made a long study of the evidence, and effected discoveries of new and important documents and witnesses In the Appendix will be found the story of the prisoner himself, as he intended to have given it to the Jury at his trial, when he was dissuaded by his Counsel from entering the box The writer claims that his discoveries complete the condemnation of the entire prosecution, and remove the " puzzles and perplexities " of earlier commentators. All that remains now is a case against the Secret Criminal system which brought about such glaring evils as are here exposed The issues to follow are in the hands of the press and public

Let us first examine if burglary was the true motive ?

The conviction of Oscar Slater as the murderer of Miss Gilchrist is based upon the assumption of his having been the alleged thief of the missing diamond brooch, and that the act of murder itself was but a secondary or adventitious affair ; a part of the crime only in so far as its execution was necessary to ensure the accomplishment of the robbery The robbery, according to this theory, was first, the murder subsidiary. The only conclusion the police, in their avowed theory of burglary, must have drawn from the tragedy in its relation to Oscar Slater was :—

(1) That Miss Gilchrist was possessed of a stock of jewellery, and

(2) that Slater was hard up and in need of money.

Nevertheless, this summary interpretation of the crime does not at all fit in with the other multitudinous details, (which, if rightly understood, unite to point the finger of suspicion in quite an opposite direction) The assailant, whoever he was, defied every prompting of reason, every calculation of premeditated criminal astuteness (He chose to enter the house during a ten-minutes' absence of the maid, a period altogether inadequate for the difficulties of access to such a well-guarded house and for the successful issue to his plans) Twice a week, on Thursdays and Sundays, the opportunity was presented him, on these off half-days of the servant, to have obtained five hours assured respite from interruption (That very day of the murder he might have had the whole afternoon, the servant having gone out on an absence of several hours' duration) Nor need he, to have achieved the paltry object accredited to him,

have carried his assault to such brutal excess
If burglary was the motive all that was required
for its easy completion was a tap on the head of
his victim to stun, insertion in the mouth of a
gag, and binding of the limbs He could then
at ease have removed the entire hoard—not the
paltry £50 worth—but actually £3,000 worth of
jewellery All that is in negation of the burglary
theory.

Further, the concentration upon the head of
the victim of so much violent smashing was not
without its significance If it be asserted that
the excess of savagery, unnecessary for burglary,
and so abhorrent in the case of an old and
defenceless lady, proceeded from some inherent
brutal impulse on the part of the assailant, the
restriction to the head and face of the blows
opposes that theory. Not the lust of savagery
but extinction of life dominated his onslaught.
The minor consideration of robbery was over-
whelmed, not by the desire, but the necessity,
to murder This, as the supreme object of the
assailant, was perceived by Lord Guthrie at the
trial, although his Lordship failed to apply
his observation to Oscar Slater It was clearly,
he said, "a case of dead men, or rather dead
women, tell no tales" That is the inevitable
conclusion to be reached by a careful study of

the facts ! And if we accept that view, mere robbery, as the motive, is quite inadequate

If we assume burglary as motive other serious difficulties are presented. When Adams rang the bell and thereby warned the murderer, at that moment busy at work, why was it he refused to desist from the violence responsible for the alarm ? It is certain that a mere robber, once he knew he was discovered, would have at once turned his attention to looking after his own safety. Not so the assailant here ! He still carried on. Nor did he attempt to leave the house until he had visited the bedroom and concluded a search of the private papers. The door had been actually opened from the outside before this man attempted to clear off. Observe with what ease he passed from the dining-room to the location of the private papers in the bedroom, signifying familiarity with the most intimate arrangements of the household. These circumstances go to show that the procuration of some document in that box of papers was as essential to the murderer's objects as his effecting the silence of the victim. He declined to leave until he had made certain that the victim not only should not survive but should be so far beyond the level of consciousness as to be unable to utter a single word—his name —to the people whom he knew to be waiting at the door. Likewise he would not depart till he secured a document.

There is this further consideration · that when Adams on the first occasion left the door and went downstairs, the assailant was presented with a clear opportunity to escape. If he had accepted that moment to make good his escape downstairs, all risk would have been obviated of interception and capture before he regained the street, in which case his identity was absolutely hidden /That golden opportunity to clear off without trace of identity—which no mere burglar would have despised, he declined to take) He remained to make sure of the silence of his victim Obviously, the paramount consideration before him was that she would " tell no tales." He was killing against time Of all the exigencies he had to think about, and which determined whether he should bolt or remain, the most dangerous was to leave the old lady in a state of partial consciousness with the faculty of speech still undestroyed If he extinguished that faculty he destroyed his own gravest risk The danger next most serious to him was the importunate people at the door—(he knew the maid had the keys and would open without pulling the bell) That, however, still offered him a chance of escape , and, as events proved, he was correct in his estimate of the alternative risks he had to face. The main inference from all this is that he feared the woman would denounce him, and if she could denounce him then he was someone who was known to her

Let us now consider the problem of the assailant's entrance, which will be shown to support the same conclusion

It was known, but not widely, that the old lady of West Princes Street was in possession of a valuable hoard of jewellery She had occupied the house for thirty years, and during that period, being well to do, she had gratified a passion for the acquisition of jewellery, in her own strange way, not for gaudy display but for accumulation within doors Her hoard had grown to be worth £3,000 These possessions were not deposited in the jewel-box she kept, which was used for the retention of her private papers and was found and opened by the assailant on the night in question The jewels were concealed with a sort of miserly prudence in the linings and interiors of garments, hung up in a bedroom wardrobe There was a story in circulation that she had collected the hoard by the questionable method of resetting stolen property This rather wicked allegation, in general circulation after her death, was rebutted at the trial of Oscar Slater Evidence was given on behalf of a firm of city jewellers proving that the stock had been legitimately acquired by purchase from their establishment. Incidentally, one may be permitted to digress upon the foolish rumours which spring up during a murder trial regarding the principals, and very often prejudice the public mind in sadly erroneous ways against the honour or truthfulness of a witness or the innocence of the accused. It was whispered also, for example, that the servant-maid, Helen Lambie, was in reality an illegitimate daughter of Miss Gilchrist. This rumour, equally false, was disposed of also at the trial. A relative of the deceased, who was interrogated upon her having heard the report, was asked these questions :—

Q   How old was Miss Gilchrist ?
A   Eighty-three.
Q   And the age of the maid ?
A   Twenty.

So much for public rumour in murder cases !

Admitting that the presence in the house of the victim of a hoard of jewellery may have received some degree of notoriety in the district, it is not to be carelessly assumed that the owner was some senile simpleton regardless of the menace of burglary.

The old lady, as a matter of fact, was very much alive to this danger and had in consequence

adopted a number of precautionary measures
insomuch that it would have been a very difficult
task indeed for any burglar to have secured
admission. Apart from the old-womanish way
of concealment inside garments—an expedient
that would not have long detained an expert
criminal—Miss Gilchrist, for protection, had
set up quite a number of alarms and traps. The
rear window had been specially secured   The
normal defences of the door had been strength-
ened by the addition of two extra locks, a bolt
and chain   It was virtually a burglar-proof
door. To cope with the more remote con-
tingency of actual intrusion, arrangements had
been made with her neighbours, the Adams
downstairs, whereby in the unlikely event of a
surprise attack she would summon their assistance by three audible knocks on the floor. That
signal was undoubtedly made by her and was
heard by the Adams on the evening of the
crime—but only after the " thud " of her fall
to the floor. This circumstance shows the
suddenness and unexpectedness of the attack ;
the old lady, in presence of her assailant being
in no fear and not giving her signal—her right
arm was found outstretched on the floor—until
after she had been felled.

From the public street access to her house
by a visitor was gained by pulling a down-

stairs bell which announced the call in the hall upstairs Here, by movement of a lever, the fastenings on the street door were released and entrance offered to the stairway which went up to her house This outer street door had been closed by the servant-girl when she went out on her newspaper errand on the night under review, so that the assailant, if he did not ring that outer bell, which would be a warning to the lonely occupant, would require three keys to get into the house This stairway was unenclosed, so that almost from her doorstep Miss Gilchrist, if she looked down, could ascertain who was coming upstairs. We have it, too, on the signed testimony of the servant girl (see White Paper 1914) that her aged mistress was so timidly apprehensive of the approach of strangers that on the occasions of the maid's absence, when summoned by the ring of the bell from the street below, Miss Gilchrist would proceed to the door, and, if still unrelieved in her anxieties as to the *bona fides* of the ascending visitor, would hastily retreat within doors and remain there unresponsive to all solicitations to open, howsoever importunate these might be On any occasion when she had gone out and forgotten her keys, Lambie declared she had on her return always found her mistress on the stair looking to see who was coming up It is

clear then that the aged lady with her £3,000
hoard of jewellery was no easy pigeon to be
plucked by any promiscuous rogue, nor might
it be supposed that any stranger had divined
all the ruses the occupant had devised to keep
intruders at bay

Knowledge of these facts disposes one to
perceive that it was difficult, if not impossible,
for any stranger to gain entrance to the house
This getting of the assailant into the house is
an absolute *sine qua non* to any acceptable
solution of the crime. The case begins with
the opening of the door—whether by Miss
Gilchrist or otherwise. If we assume the
assailant to have been known to her the problem
disappears He would ring below, she would
release the outer door, inspect him as he
ascended the stair, and knowing him, admit him.
But if we assume a stranger, such as Oscar
Slater, there would be detention at the door
and the use of false keys would be necessary,
which would have put the old lady wise and
caused her to signal for the Adams The
police did not attempt before the Jury, as
they ought to have done, to offer any solution of
the mystery of access. Like so much else
in the case they conveniently solved the problem
by ignoring its existence No evidence whatever was submitted at the trial to show how

a complete stranger, Oscar Slater, slipped past the defences, nor was there revealed the significant fact that no marks of forcing were found on the door (The Jury was not instructed upon these all-important matters) As the starting point in their investigations, the Jury accepted the presence in the house of the accused In so assuming the burglar's entrance, the whole case was begged) The short time taken over the crime showed clearly that the intruder was not detained at the door—a circumstance which suggests that the assailant was not a stranger In the absence of disclosure to the Jury of these important details, the Lord Advocate, who prosecuted, described the victim as " an aged and defenceless lady ")Defenceless she was, physically, we agree, but not strategically That statement insinuated that the defenceless lady was easy game for a man like Slater to kill and rob, which might indeed be true if any possible means could be suggested by which he could approach her These, however, were entirely wanting.

We return now to the night of the murder and to a closer examination of the incidents which preceded and succeeded the discovery of the tragedy It is not improper to suggest that after the warning at the door, given to the maid by Adams on her return from her errand,

✱ Park reprises many points made in ACD (1912).
i.e., ACD's work, in various ways, made Park's possible.

she should have had all her wits about her
to be ready to challenge any intruder who should,
upon her entrance, disclose his presence) The
lighted bedroom told her further that someone
might have entered the house since she left
it ten minutes earlier. (Lambie, standing in
the hall, undoubtedly saw the man leave the
bedroom and enter the lobby) Strange to say,
such an incident produced upon her no sign of
alarm   She made no challenge   She did not
seek to detain or question the man.   In all
the circumstances of the moment, highly pregnant
with possibilities of unusual happenings, (this
attitude of apathy and unconcern was incom-
prehensible unless we assume that the appearance or knowledge of the man suggested to
her mind the absence of sinister motive or
evil design on his part.) Most servants in such
a quandary would surely have been greatly
agitated   Mr. Adams, too, seemed remiss in
allowing a man to leave the house whom he
must have assumed to be the author of the
disturbances which occasioned his presence at the
door and had alarmed his sisters   This omission
to act was brought to his notice during the
later extradition proceedings at New York
against Slater at which he was a witness.   Mr.
Adams offered to the Court this explanation—
that it was Christmas time, that from his

manner the man seemed to have a right to be there, and that, in fact, he seemed to be a male acquaintance of Miss Gilchrist) He further declared that the man's gentlemanly appearance did not at all suggest to him a burglar Lord Guthrie, presiding at the trial in Edinburgh, also saw the omission and expressed his regret that " he had not slammed that door." The *Glasgow Herald* of 22nd December, 1908, the morning after the crime, reporting an interview with Mr Adams, stated that the witness thought the assailant " so respectable in appearance, I just imagined him to be a friend of Miss Gilchrist or the servant."

These incidents unite in support of the conclusion that the assailant was not any common intruder or burglar who had thrust his way into the house. The earliest descriptions of the assailant's appearance, as observed by Lambie and Adams, speak of him as young and of a most gentlemanly bearing We observe from files of the local press of those days that a number of suspects in custody and shown to these eye-witnesses,* were rejected as not gentlemanly enough and not youthful enough. Oscar Slater might be described as not in the least youthful nor gentlemanly-looking. He

*Adams admitted at New York he had been shown four arrested suspects before leaving Glasgow

was at that time a man thirty-eight years of age (Lambie and Adams said their man was about twenty-five or thirty) and he was, we are told, more of a sporting type and common rather than attractive He was indeed just the sort of man upon whom, had she observed his figure on her stairs, Miss Gilchrist would have exercised that little plan of running indoors and turning on all the special fastenings of the door Thus, if a stranger such as Oscar Slater, be assumed as the author of the murder, and robbery to be the motive, the whole circumstances of the crime are simply impossible of explanation

Other incidents of the night add weight to these conclusions. Before leaving on her nightly mission to fetch the newspaper, the maid had occasion to enter the dining-room, where she observed her mistress seated comfortably near the fireplace in the act of reading a magazine. She was wearing her spectacles. After the occurrence of the tragedy, the magazine was discovered lying on the table with the spectacles neatly folded beside it, just as any careful reader momentarily interrupted, but with every intention to return to the page in resumption of the reading, would have done. (This circumstance shows conclusively that the victim, immediately before the attack, had been temporarily interrupted by some wholly peaceful summons and had not been suddenly taken by surprise and pounced upon—this latter assumption being an indispensable factor to any supposition that Slater was the intruder. Nor can it be doubted that any attempt to force the door would have led Miss Gilchrist to at once put into operation her prearranged signal with the Adams below. That signal was three knocks on her floor. These knocks were not heard till after a great " thud "—obviously the fall of the victim to the floor at the delivery of the first savage blow. The entire circumstances, we submit, are explicable only upon one ground, which each step in our investigations renders clearer · that the assailant knew the victim and that he was admitted by her voluntarily and without suspicion to the doomed abode

At the trial of Slater none of these further illuminating details was mentioned to the Jury. One man there was, however, who understood them and read their significance. This was the the New York Solicitor of Oscar Slater, who represented the prisoner at the extradition proceedings in that city in January, 1909. This gentleman, when he had the servant-girl under cross-examination, obliged her to admit the strangeness of these circumstances regarding the entrance of the assailant, and then

Extradition hearing

when he had reduced her to the embarrassment of offering some suitable explanation, he shot out at her this tremendously important question —
" Who opened the door ? "
The answer was .—
" *Miss Gilchrist must have opened the door* "
That admission by the servant, who knew every detail of the victim's life and her ways of dealing with visitors of all kinds, supplied the key which unlocked the whole mystery of the crime

The inevitable sequel to such an admission in the Court of New York came from Slater's solicitor. This was to press the point that the murder had not taken place at the door, as might be expected if a stranger entered, but at the dining-room fireplace, a considerable distance, the girl admitted, from the door, through the lobby (18 feet) and the length of the room. The answer to all this range-finding by the solicitor was rather unsatisfactory, and then he came closer to the target with this question —
" Were there ever any *male* acquaintances of the deceased who called upon her ? "
The answer was in the negative Repeating the question, she replied —" Well, lady friends There were two nieces who called " This denial regarding male visitors, let it be interpolated,

was an evasion of the truth In the precognition of her evidence, taken after her return to Glasgow by the Glasgow agent of Oscar Slater, and before the trial in Edinburgh, the girl admitted that there were such callers at the house and specifically mentioned one

It cannot be doubted then that the servant maid had a clear view of the real meaning of the tragedy, and that she knew it was no stranger who had secured admittance to the house The meaning of it all was simply this. Miss Gilchrist attended personally to the summons, opened the door herself, admitted her visitor after reconnoitring him and accompanied him through the lobby to her seat near the fireplace in the dining-room when the first fatal blow was struck. Furthermore, the man who passed up the stairs did not occasion to the vigilant occupant any alarm as to her safety when she stood at the door to follow her invariable practice of seeing who it was that approached ; nor did he cause her to put into operation that little precautionary plan of hers to retire within doors and wait the servant's return Lastly, she did not sound the prearranged signal of distress to the Adams until surprised and felled at the fireplace. It is indisputable that the victim was on friendly terms with the man whom she admitted and who was to become her murderer)This, of course, could in no way apply to the alien Jew who was the object of the official accusation

Do we know anything of this mysterious and tragic visitor ?

Upon the major issue to be resolved—the identity of the assailant and the motive which brought him to the house of the victim—the foregoing circumstances unite to point the finger of suspicion in a direction away entirely from the stranger, Oscar Slater) The unexplained inactivity of the police in pursuing the obvious line of investigation which pointed to a man known to the deceased, and departing from it to go after a trail which disagreed with the whole circumstances of the tragedy, would leave us baffled and bewildered were it not for an important sequel to the conviction of Slater which ensued several years subsequent to the trial This was the revelation of inner police secrets by one of the officers engaged in the work of investigation This man was perhaps the ablest detective in the Glasgow force His abilities were so well recognised that he had been chosen by the Lord Provost of Glasgow to aid the Dundee police in the elucidation of a mys- terious murder on Tayside This was Lieutenant John T Trench, a King's Medallist—for exem- plary and meritorious police services The revelations by this officer formed the subject of the secret inquiry before referred to Lieutenant Trench in the year 1914 deemed it expedient to speak out. He had experienced in the Dundee murder case a series of disconcerting mistakes by witnesses in attempts to identify a suspect which, but for the straightforward efforts of this officer, would have led to a recurrence of the blunder under review. Trench succeeded in tracing in a pawnshop in Antwerp indisputable evidence that the suspect, identified by a dozen witnesses as having been seen at Dundee at the time of the tragedy, had in reality been in Antwerp, sleeping out at nights without residence, and that, luckily for his neck, he had pawned a waistcoat there. After this experience he was naturally awake to the dangers of this class of evidence, and he then turned his attention to the Slater case, a conviction which, to journalists and others, he had never ceased to denounce.

For his own safety, Trench decided to approach the Secretary for Scotland. He well knew that the police system insists upon the inviolate observance of secrecy, and ruthlessly visits punishments upon all who disclose its secrets, even in a case where blundering might have existed. Trench declared that in regard to Slater there had occurred the gravest irregulari-

ties in the procedure and preparation of the
case, and that evidence which proved the
innocence of Slater and destroyed the prosecution had been withheld from the Jury. Realising
the difficulties of his position, Trench decided to
utilise the medium of a Glasgow solicitor for
his approach to the Scottish Secretary. This
solicitor, appreciating also the difficulties of
the officer and wishful to safeguard him, indicated to the Secretary that Trench was prepared
to make serious disclosures, but first demanded
and obtained a guarantee that, for any disclosure of official secrets, Trench would not
suffer victimisation In the end, however, the
officer was dismissed and suffered the loss of
pension and all privileges he had earned.

Copies of documents and statements of witnesses unseen by the Jury were then forwarded
to the Secretary for Scotland. Concerning the
important question now before us—that of
the knowledge of the servant girl as to the
identity of the murderer and whether on the
occurrence of the tragedy she had confessed his
name, Trench made this personal statement.
On the night of the murder Lambie, the servant,
he declared, had run straightaway to the house
near by of a niece, named Miss Burrell, and had
there confessed to the name of the man whom she
had seen to leave the house Miss Burrell was

stated to have rebuked her and asked her to be
very careful The officer further declared that
in response to instructions from his superiors,
he had proceeded on Wednesday, 23rd December,
two days after the crime, to the house of Miss
Burrell, and from the lips of that lady herself
had obtained full confirmation of the accusation
said to have been made to her by Lambie

The Secretary for Scotland could scarcely
avoid dealing with revelations of such startling
importance, and that gentleman thereupon was
forced to act. He appointed the late Mr J
Gardner Millar, Sheriff of Lanarkshire, to sit as
Commissioner and enquire into the revelations,
but with a strange satire upon the avowed desire
to elucidate the truth, he ordered that the
Commissioner should not enquire into the
conduct of the trial—a reservation which virtually reduced to negligibility the Commissioner's
pretended powers of investigation It appeared
also that the Commissioner was to sit in private,
that no shorthand writer was to be present,
and that the witnesses were not to be sworn;
while the prisoner was to be unrepresented.
To put the coping stone on the comedy, the
Commissioner (vide his subsequent report) wrote
to the Fiscal and Chief Constable, the two
highest officials responsible for the preparation
of the case, and therefore the two men whose

reputations were at stake, asking them for their assistance, and, in the official report, gratefully acknowledged that they had " *promised to help him* " Probably in the history of criminal jurisprudence no such judicial farce was ever staged It was surprising that the press was unable to stop this pretence at satisfying the public conscience, while, at the same time, doing nothing to right the wrong. It is true that the London *Times* entered a protest,* but the farce proceeded, and we shall see, in the course of our review of its deliberations, the extra-ordinary comedy that was enacted For our present purpose, it is sufficient that in the locked secret apartment set apart for the Commissioner Miss Burrell, the niece of the deceased, and the police superintendents responsible for the conduct of the case, who were stated to have despatched Trench on the mission to that lady's house of testing the authenticity of Lambie's alleged confession, succeeded admirably in contradicting one another. The Superintendents denied or forgot having sent Trench to Miss Burrell's That lady frankly admitted the call of the officer, but gave an emphatic denial to his statements regarding Lambie's confession The servant-girl also, when before the Commissioner, denied the story of her alleged confession, although it is to be remembered that at New

*Locally the Glasgow *Evening News* joined in this protest

York she left little doubt that Miss Gilchrist knew the assailant and had added an evasive statement, afterwards contradicted by herself, that no male acquaintance ever called on the deceased (The Commissioner, in his official report, paid Lambie the compliment that she seemed to be desirous of speaking the truth) To him she declared this story regarding her alleged confession about another man to be news to her, and was very much astonished, she said, to hear it. This statement and the compliment paid her by the Commissioner as to her truthfulness simply illustrated the farce of the proceedings and the abuse of facts permitted by the Commissioner in the absence of cross-examination) As a matter of fact, the late Lieutenant Trench had earlier made known to Slater's agent this confession of Lambie's , and the Solicitor had traced her out in a Lanarkshire village and taxed her with it) At the very moment when she was expressing her surprise to the Commissioner and he was patting her on the back for her truthfulness, there was an entry in the journal of the law agent indicating his tracing, discovery and challenge of Lambie * This, the writer personally saw at the time Had this farcical tribunal permitted cross - examination there would have been a different story to tell

*See statements in White Paper by Lieut Trench and Miss Burrell

But even at this secret inquiry there was corroboration for Trench of a remarkable character This was a statement from Inspector Cameron, a brother officer to Trench. Cameron openly told the Commissioner that he recollected Trench having been sent to the house of Miss Burrell, and that upon his return therefrom, Trench had reported to him that he had obtained from that lady full confirmation of the confession by Lambie regarding another man (Cameron gave the exact name) as the murderer Observe now the attitude of the Commissioner ' No pats on the back for Cameron ' The Commissioner added in his report an interpolation, obviously his own : " Of course, that was only hearsay from Trench " It was, we reply, nothing of the sort : It was first-hand communication. It was given, too, immediately the officer returned to headquarters. Obviously that interpolation was added simply to water down the strength of the confirmation by Cameron. Nor did the Commissioner take steps to get to the bottom of the contradictions here It is clear he ought at least to have recalled the two police superintendents and said to them : " It is proved by Trench that he made the call at the house of Miss Burrell which you forget or deny You must refresh your memories and tell me for what purpose you despatched this officer . I

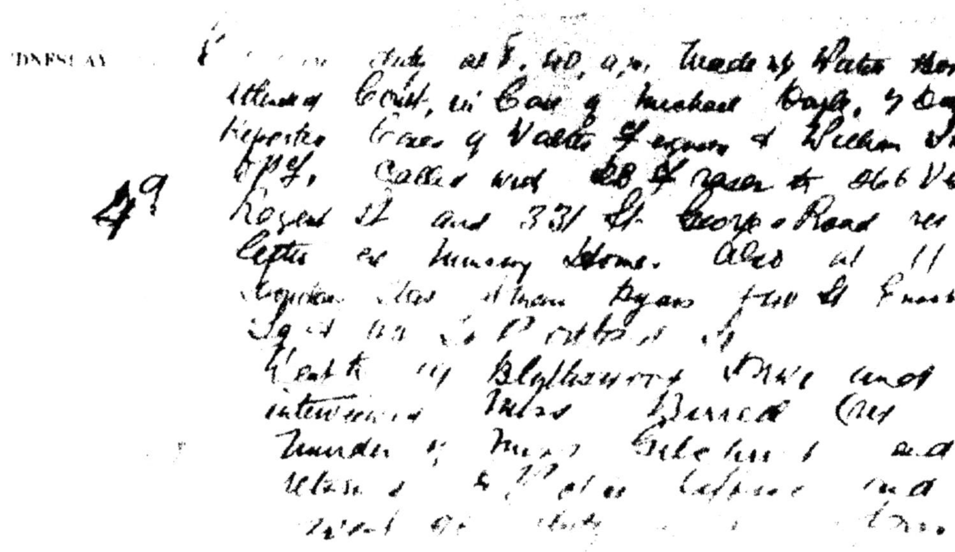

4º

[handwritten diary entry, largely illegible]

EXCERPT FROM TRENCH'S OFFICIAL DIARY

recently taken shows the officer's record in his own handwriting, of used
ber 1908 when he made his official call at Mrs Luard's address to Mrs
aperters at the inquiry of why denied or forgot having sent him there
there was no official record of the call

want from you his official report on the call "*
But this gentleman was not to inquire into the
conduct of the police, and his obedience was
most exemplary   A still more serious omission
by him in regard to a witness will be revealed
in the chapter which relates to Mary Barrowman

These remarkable disclosures by Lieutenant
Trench concerning the identification by the
servant-maid of a man other than Oscar Slater
as the murderer do not happen to be really
new Representatives of the Press in contact
with the details of the crime were well aware at
the time that a development of some such
character had ensued (Such, of course, could
not be published, and was only naively hinted
at in the Press Confirmation of this is still
available from the local Press reports of the
time.

The Glasgow Herald of 23rd December, 1908,
for instance, stated : (This is the day Trench
says he called at Burrell's) :—

" Certain circumstances would seem to
point to the likelihood of Miss Gilchrist herself having attended the door when the
stranger called. When the servant left the

*We reproduce on opposite page a photograph of Lieutenant
Trench's official diary (still extant), showing the entry of his call
at Miss Burrell's   The " 2 " on the margin indicates the 2d
for his tram fare expended on the mission which was reimbursed
by his superiors

house to go for a newspaper her mistress was sitting in front of the dining-room fire reading a magazine. She was wearing glasses at the time After the murder was discovered the magazine was found lying open on the table and on the top of it lay the spectacles as if they had been carefully placed there The theory is advanced that on hearing the door-bell ring she took these off and went to answer the summons. There was no evidence of a struggle in the hall, and if it is assumed that the old lady opened the door, she must have returned to the dining-room and taken up a position close to the chair which she had shortly before vacated. The large table in the dining-room had evidently been pushed aside and the murderous attack made upon Miss Gilchrist while she was standing upon the hearth-rug in front of the fire ''

Again on Saturday, 26th December, the same paper says :—

  " Whatever way investigations are tending *it has been learned that the police have not departed from the opinion that the assailant was known to the victim* ''

On Wednesday, 23rd December, the day of Trench's call at Miss Burrell's, the *Glasgow News* published a most ominous paragraph in confirmation of the new development, and prepared its readers for a sensational outcome that might take place at any moment. The *News* inferred that not the brooch but the Will was now concerned.

No unprejudiced mind can possibly emerge from these considerations relative to the girl's alleged confession without a conviction that Trench made good the foundation of his case, and that the Commissioner made no effort whatever to clear the issues of its ambiguities It is noticeable in the " White Paper," which constituted the Commissioner's report, that the unassailable corroboration by Detective Cameron was accorded a remote back page—a circumstance which trapped two leading Scottish newspapers into a declaration that Trench was uncorroborated. The Commissioner, in the formulation of his report, observed neither order nor sequence ; he flung in his statements without regard to value or subject. It was noticed, too—the report having been written in long-hand from dictation by the Commissioner—that the witnesses, educated and uneducated, used always similar flamboyant phrases—" Absolutely false ; absolutely untrue ! " The inquiry, which was supposed to clear up all mysteries, only added another mystery—how such a farce came to be palmed off on the British public. The report of the Commissioner was printed and tabled in the House of Commons   Forty letters were sent by Slater's solicitor to members of that august assemblage, pointing out the inconsistencies of the document itself ; the ample proofs it afforded that there had been irregularities in the procedure, together with suppression of evidence Of the entire forty, only a single member asked a question. Mr. McKinnon Wood, the Secretary for Scotland, declared to the House that the statements of the officer had been " carefully " inquired into—and there was an end of it ! We shall see further as we proceed the alleged " carefulness " of the inquiry !

We pass now to a consideration of the coming into the case of the prisoner, Oscar Slater. His appearance in the police inquiries and the acceptance of him as the probable murderer, corresponded with the superficial theory of burglary which had been set up within two hours of the discovery of the crime, as set forth in the official document already alluded to, a document which was itself inaccurate in vital details regarding the crime.   Slater's appearance turned the attention of the police away from further clues. Once a suspect is on hand it is natural to abandon work on the crime and turn a detective staff upon the movements, etc., of a

particular man   And this is just what transpired

To go back a little, one of the earliest steps
undertaken by the police was the preparation for
circulation and publication of a " description "
of the assailant, so far as could be ascertained from
the meagre details which Mr Adams and the girl
Lambie were able to provide. The emerging
result was the vaguest "description." These witnesses were able to speak only to a man of " from
twenty-five to thirty years of age, five feet
seven inches or eight inches in height, thin,
clean-shaven, and wore a long grey overcoat
and dark cap." The description, applied generally in Glasgow, might have brought in ten
thousand men.   Accordingly, it was not surprising that the publication of such a paltry index
to the identification of a murderer should have
produced intangible results The police themselves appeared to have been baffled

However, later in the week, a development
occurred when a third eye-witness came forward
in the person of a little message girl, fourteen
years of age, named Mary Barrowman, who made
a fresh statement. Mary's mother had been
talking to a detective officer resident in the
same flat, and this was responsible for Mary's
coming into the case The mother informed
the officer that Mary had been out late on

Monday evening, and on returning home had told her of a murder that had taken place in the city, and added some information as to her having been there and observed a man. Before going further with the statement made by this girl, it might be observed that as she claimed to have been at the scene of the murder a second time, at 10 p.m., to learn then of the tragedy and was late in returning to her home, there was a strangeness in her reticence to the police officers who were on duty in West Princes Street keeping the crowds in order which had assembled at the house of the victim. She told no one at that time of these experiences earlier in the evening concerning the man whom she now declared to have seen coming from the house. Leave that aside, however, in the meanwhile Mary made a statement two days after the crime to the effect that while passing along West Princes Street on an errand for her employer, a bootmaker, when near to the house of Miss Gilchrist, she had observed a man to run from the doorway and pass " pretty close " to her She declared that she had turned and followed the fugitive for some distance—a remarkable act surely, on the part of an errand girl When asked for an explanation of it, her inconsequent reply was that she thought him running to catch a tram car. It is to be recalled that just after the time of her passing the house of Miss Gilchrist, when the man ran out of the stairway, and her return from following the fugitive there were four people on the street—Mr. Adams, his two sisters and the servant This quartette declared that no one was to be seen near Miss Gilchrist's house, and Barrowman likewise declared that no one was to be seen by her.

It was a dark, rainy December night, yet this little girl professed in that instant of the man flying past her to have been able to take in the lineaments of his face, to observe the kind of hat and coat he wore, and also to see that his boots were brown-coloured From the details furnished by this girl, a second description of a wanted man was prepared by the police It reached the columns of the evening newspapers on Friday, 25th December—the day when Slater happened to have completed the arrangements for departure, upon which, as will be shown, he had been engaged for several weeks This fresh description spoke of a man twenty-five to thirty years of age, tall and thin, wearing a fawn waterproof and brown boots.* There was also a detail indicating that the man had a twisted nose.

*There was at that moment in the Northern police office, *vide* Press reports, a suspect, who was released, with fawn-coloured waterproof and brown boots

Such a description did not help the police; it was so much in conflict with that furnished by Lambie and Adams as to give them only added perplexity. In their dilemma they did a very proper thing they issued a document which was forwarded to all other police staffs (but, be it noticed, was kept back from the Press and public), requesting officers to be on the look-out for two men · (1) one spoken to by Lambie and Adams, and (2) by Barrowman. In some of the issues of that document it was declared specifically that officers were not to confound *the two men* spoken to by Barrowman and Lambie—a perfectly proper document to issue ' But how came it, we ask, that these two not-to-be-confounded men resolved themselves at last into the one man—Oscar Slater ? Explanation of that mystery is reserved for later reference. So far as present purposes are concerned, Barrowman has complicated the issues seriously. Not one, but two men are now to be traced and found !

The issue to the public of these two "descriptions," so bald of details, was unproductive of result The public, meanwhile, were not troubling much about these cryptic descriptions. The diamond brooch had seized the popular imagination, and the hue and cry of the streets was all for a burglar with a brooch. And it was this hue and cry that dragged Slater into the case ! During the days immediately succeeding the tragedy this German Jew had been openly offering for sale in a number of public-houses, gambling clubs, and billiard-rooms he frequented a pawn-ticket for a diamond brooch (Slater had arrived in Glasgow from London just eight weeks before the tragedy, and had at a later date taken up residence at Charing Cross, not far distant from the house of Miss Gilchrist He was a man without occupation or reputation, lived by gambling and card-playing, and far from opulent. There were other charges of immoral living against him, not proved, but thrown at him at the trial and made the most of by the Lord Advocate, concerning which, however, a clause in a secret police document declared that it could not have been proved. He had apparently found Glasgow too hard a nut to crack in the extraction of money, and had decided to re-try his luck in New York, where he had been resident in earlier years. The announcements of his intentions to return there were open; he did everything cleanly and above board in his preparations for going. He had arranged to bring from London a party to take over his flat and to continue the instalments he had contracted to pay on the hired furniture in his house. The hour of his departure was timed precisely with the arrival of the people from London to take over his flat, and at noon on the day of his departure from Glasgow, he had actually seen them installed in his house. At this point in our story Slater is getting ready to depart, he has been at the Cunard Company's office and at Cook's office, giving his own name and address in Glasgow, to book passages for America / As a last resource in picking up some extra money for the journey to New York, he is offering for sale a pawn-ticket for a diamond brooch, an article rather difficult for sale as he had previously procured on it in cash the sum of £50.

This exposure for sale of a pawn-ticket for a diamond brooch in these days of excitement in Glasgow over the murder and robbery, naturally drew upon him the suspicion that the brooch was the very article stolen from the house of the murdered lady / On Christmas night —twenty-four hours after Slater had generously sent off to his father and mother in Germany a gift of a five-pound note—a man named Allan McLean, a cycle agent in Glasgow, walked into the Central Police Chambers and reported that a party, a foreign Jew, whom he knew only by the name of " Oscar," had been exhibiting for sale in certain clubs in the city a pawn-ticket for a diamond brooch / This was wonderful news for the police—a red-hot trail to proceed upon at last. From the moment that this report of McLean's reached them, all else concerning the tragedy—including the idea of a man known to the victim and who had been admitted by her—evaporated and disappeared. Never again was there a suggestion of a police hunt for a man corresponding with this interpretation of the crime The hunt for Slater, the "Oscar" of McLean, was inaugurated and never relinquished, despite repeated blunderings. Even the leading newspapers forgot all that they had published concerning the man being known to the victim, and joined in the sensations of tracing, pursuing, capturing and convicting this new quarry

And what of the man supposed to have been accused by the servant-girl as being the murderer ? Not another word Lieutenant Trench made this statement to the Commissioner in the 1914 inquiry · " Detective Cameron and I went along to Miss Burrell's house on 9th January, 1909, by instructions of Superintendent Ord. I went to Miss Burrell's and Cameron went to another family of Burrell's to warn them not to say anything about the story of the man accused by Lambie, as it would do him (the man so accused) no good and there was nothing in it." *There is an entry in Trench's official diary (still extant) to show this visit.* Detective Cameron admitted

being sent to the Burrell's, but told the Commissioner it was about another matter   We
leave the business there

On Christmas night the police decided to
arrest Slater on the strength of the report of his
having a pawn-ticket for a diamond brooch.) To
make capture doubly sure, action was delayed
until Slater would be likely to have entered his
house for the night.   On arrival at his residence,
about 9 p m., or thereby, they made the startling
discovery that their bird had flown. Inquiries
among neighbours and at the door of Slater's
house revealed that the wanted man, a little
earlier, had left his apartments and gone off in a
cab to the Central Station This information
was chiefly obtained from a German maid,
Catherine Schmalz, who had been left behind.
This girl had been dismissed from his service on
account of his leaving for America, and she had
remained to be of assistance to the newcomers
from London. The officers engaged in the
quest for him ascertained that their man had left
for Liverpool although there appears to have been
some bungling, and they at first thought he had
set off for London. He was accompanied
by his mistress, the French woman, Antoine.
This was further tremendous news for the
police. With the same incautious precipitation

which, on the night of the crime, had caused them to jump to robbery as the motive, they now judged the man with the diamond brooch to be a fugitive from justice

THE PURSUIT OF OSCAR SLATER

While Slater was composedly whirling his way to Liverpool on the night train all unconscious of the movements at police headquarters in Glasgow to effect his arrest, the authorities, convinced beyond doubt that this was their man, were not remiss in attending to their duties of the moment They regarded his departure from Glasgow as an affair of sudden decision and preparation , that the fugitive had perceived the closing round him of the net of suspicion and had given them the slip by an hour or two's forestalment of inevitable arrest Meanwhile, the pressing problem was the location in Glasgow of the pawnshop where the all-important brooch was on deposit, the identification of which before further steps were taken was a primary necessity From habitués of sporting clubs which had been nightly frequented by the suspect, it was ascertained that Slater had been an associate of one, Cameron, known colloquially in Glasgow as "the Moudie," and possibly from that quarter it was thought they might procure more definite information concerning the pawn-ticket and the whereabouts of the pawn office.

Without loss of time officers were despatched to the home of Cameron, and the occupier knocked up out of bed in the early hours of the morning. The disturbed sleeper was interrogated as to his knowledge of the suspected article of jewellery. From this party the police received confirmation that their man was in actual possession of a pawn-ticket for a diamond brooch and had attempted to effect its disposal in Glasgow. Cameron further confided that he had personally taken a hand in the business of the attempted sale.

Then came this unexpected thunderbolt of news. The brooch, he said, was not any stolen article . it was the actual property of Slater, and had been brought by him to Glasgow when he came from London two months before. They would find it, he added, in the pawnshop of Mr. Liddell, Sauchiehall Street. This was the first of a long series of cold douches the Glasgow authorities were to receive in damping the ardour of their irrepressible quest.

To test this disconcerting piece of news, detective officers were detailed first thing in the morning to proceed to the pawn office to which they had been directed by Cameron. To ensure unmistaken identification of the brooch the servant-girl, Lambie, was asked to accompany them Mr Liddell at once produced from his repositories the article covered by the ticket issued to Oscar Slater.   The girl, at first glance, emphatically rejected the produced brooch   No second look was needed.   She explained that the stolen brooch was set with a single row of stones   There were three on the pawned article Still more to rid the situation of doubt and to scotch the supposed clue against Slater, Mr Liddell exhibited his deposit book, which showed that the brooch had been pawned on 18th November, or four clear weeks *before* the murder, and that it had not in the interval left his premises   Another little innocent coincidence, of which there were many in this case, may here be interpolated ! Slater, on the very day of the tragedy received, as the last instalment the broker was prepared to give on the brooch, the sum of £30   And yet he was described by the Lord Advocate to the Jury as gasping and panting on the night of the murder to find money anywhere, anyhow.

The brooch clue against Slater, at the moment of that disclosure, fell dead, and its existence ought never again to have troubled the police. The elements of suspicion which had drawn Slater very properly within the orbit of police inquiry, had been swept away) However suggestive, the possession by Slater of a pawn-ticket for a brooch was shown to have been but an innocuous coincidence, remarkable perhaps, but still only one of Fate's chance throws of the dice Slater, from the moment the officers put their eyes on Liddell's deposit book, stood exculpated of every implication of guilt ; and the efforts to capture him should have instantly ceased

Nevertheless, these energetic officers of Glasgow refused to let Slater go. Trained sleuth hounds may be pardoned for excessive zeal in hanging on to an unexhausted trail of suspicion, but when that trail obviously leads into a *cul-de-sac* of innocence they ought to know when to retire gracefully. Incredible as it may seem, the collapse of the suspicious clue effected no change of attitude, no diminution of activity to run Slater to earth. The breakdown did not even appear to warn the authorities of the dangers of appearances or coincidences They went on—and the most amazing thing, as we shall see, is that the ground for following him across the seas was that self-same exposed and exploded clue of the brooch

Sir Arthur Conan Doyle long ago most cogently pointed out* that the further action taken in

*" The Case of Oscar Slater " (Hodder & Stoughton, 1912)

regard to Slater, ending in his conviction for the murder, was a logical absurdity For a man to be involved in an atmosphere of suspicion by reason of some isolated circumstance which, upon examination, proved to be only a coincidence, and in the end for it to be brought out that this wrong man was nevertheless the right man, constituted an absolute miracle in criminal investigation Slater, after the brooch clue failed, returned to the *status quo* of every other man in Glasgow.

It is to be strictly observed, lest there be misapprehension on the point, that at the moment when the brooch clue failed not another scrap of evidence against him was known That which finally determined the verdict against him—evidence of alleged identification by the eye-witnesses—was not at that stage available Slater had gone from Glasgow, and these eye-witnesses did not see him until the end of January, or nearly a month later, in New York

Ponder the problem from another angle ! A little reflection might have informed the police that the act of exposing openly for sale a pawn-ticket for a diamond brooch while the streets of Glasgow were ringing with the hue and cry for a man with a brooch or pawn-ticket, betrayed innocence rather than guilt. The police, in their after-accusations, were not slow to throw mud at Slater's character, and to impute to him the cunning of watching the house of Miss Gilchrist for two months before risking the crime. Yet, here, in this deliberate exposure publicly of the pawn-ticket after the crime they ascribed to him the mentality of a lunatic, who walked the streets of Glasgow and importuned strangers to buy—a passport for himself to the gallows.

We return to the activities of the police and find them still red-hot on the track of Oscar Slater, the supposed fugitive. Upon what grounds now, it may be asked ? Inconceivable, surely, that the exploded brooch clue still haunted their minds and constrained their action ! Yes, that self-same false and disproved clue of the diamond brooch was the urge of their pursuit. By this time one might have conjectured that " Brooch " had become anathema to the Glasgow authorities, or at least only to be whispered by their official instructors in the tutoring of novice detectives to beware the pitfalls of coincidences in clue investigation. No, they still clasped the brooch. And now we are about to reveal one more tragic blunder which, for the good name of the police and the safety of the necks of the community, we hope is unique in the history of criminal investigation.

For the moment we leave aside the question of Slater's movements, whether open or concealed, as a fugitive or otherwise. He has arrived at Liverpool in the early hours of the morning, slept at the North Western Hotel, where, be it noted, he inscribed on the official register his name · "Oscar Slater, Glasgow", has visited the Cunard Company's office, told the clerk he had come from Glasgow; and in the name of Otto Sando ("O.S." being on his luggage), paid in Scotch bank-notes for his berth on the *Lusitania*, leaving that day He sailed for New York on Saturday, 26th December, and was midway across the Atlantic when the Glasgow authorities come on the scene again, this time with a cabled message to the New York police, of which the following is the full text* :—

> "Arrest Otto Sando second cabin Lusitania wanted in connection with the murder of Marion Gilchrist at Glasgow. He has a twisted nose. *Search him and the woman who is his travelling companion for pawn-tickets.*"

At this stage earlier critics, Sir Arthur Conan Doyle and others, have confessed their inability to explain upon what grounds the arrest of Slater at New York was ordered and effected They could not understand it at all. The

*From London "Daily Telegraph," 4th January, 1909

brooch clue being dead, what suspicion could it
be the police were pursuing ?   Conjecture
could scarce find a foothold for suggestion.
The publication, however, of the text of the
official cablegram sets aside all speculation and
mystery.   It was simply a stupendous blunder.
But there it is ; the message has brought the
New York police into activity ; the consequences of the blunder are operating. The
incoming *Lusitania* is stopped and boarded by
a party of officers.   The wanted passenger is
searched out and interrogated upon his possession of a pawn-ticket in connection with a
murder in Glasgow.   Slater confesses ignorance
of any murder, but, by great good luck for
himself, happens still to have in his pocket the
wanted pawn-ticket.   It is produced   He explains that it had no connection whatever with
any crime, that the brooch was his own property, bought by himself some years before in
London as a present for his accompanying
passenger, Antoine, who confirms   To establish
his *bona fides* he does even more When the
extradition proceedings come up later, his
solicitor produces a New York jeweller, who
confesses the repair of the article to Slater on
the occasion of his last visit to New York two
years before.   He described it as an English
article, " a very peculiar thing " in its setting.

He remembered it so well he was able to make
a sketch of it   The girl, Lambie, also told the
Court that the brooch in the pawnshop covered
by the ticket in Slater's possession was not that
of her mistress. Things go from bad to worse
for the Glasgow authorities, and their repre-
sentative in New York perceives it too.

The prosecution, without however confessing
to the New York Court there had been
a mistake in arresting him on the clue of
the pawn-ticket, then goes on the line of
attempting to prove that Slater was the man
who ran out of the house of the victim on the
night of the murder Proceedings are long
drawn-out   Slater is penniless. He parted with
his gold watch to pay for his defence , and then
he intimated, as before stated, his readiness to
go back to Scotland and stand his trial

There is still more of the brooch blunder to
be revealed. We understand that in such a case
where extradition is desired a police authority
may not act directly, but must first submit to the
Crown reasons for asking for the arrest and
extradition. We believe this to have been done
in the Slater case,* and that the information so
supplied to the Crown regarding Slater's brooch
was ambiguous, and possibly led the higher

*The depositions tabled in the New York Extradition Court
bore the signature of the Under Secretary for the Home Department, and were certified by the Foreign Office

authorities into the error of petitioning for the extradition of Slater on the theory that the brooch in his possession referred to the missing brooch, the property of the victim

The author does not definitely commit himself to these views, but certainly a statement of evidence available against Slater was prepared by the Glasgow police for higher authorities at that time, and this document contained the following reference to the brooch :—

> " That he is known to be a judge of jewellery, particularly diamonds, and *has a diamond brooch pawned for £50*, and may have come to hear of the fact that the late Miss Gilchrist had a large quantity of jewellery in the house through the book-makers in the Sloper Club."

We leave it to the judgment of readers whether that was a proper statement of the truth on the question of the brooch.   " That he has a diamond brooch pawned for £50 "—a most ambiguous phrase which might very readily prejudice an official of a higher department, to whom such a document had been submitted, for consideration before action, into the supposition that the pawned brooch in Slater's possession was the property of the murdered lady.* If it was

*The Glasgow press were giving publicity at this time to statements of a similar kind, one or two suggesting that it was actually Miss Gilchrist's brooch

intended, in fact, to convey the impression that the brooch was the personal property of Slater, its inclusion in a document of evidence against him as a suspect was valueless and inept, the brooch clue being then tested and "dead."

What happened at the trial of Slater in connection with this "die-hard" brooch clue? Nothing Here, neither Judge nor Jury was informed of the mistake in the arrest of the prisoner on the false clue of the diamond brooch The Jury, if information had been passed to it of the blundering over the brooch must have inevitably dismissed the case.

It is rather remarkable that Lord Guthrie, who presided, scented out the blunder, but just stopped short of getting right home with a demand for explanation. We get this from the evidence at the trial Inspector Pyper was in the box This question was put to him by the Judge —

" Do you know whether, at the time that the warrant was issued for Slater's apprehension, it was known that the diamond brooch which he had pawned was not the same as that which was missing ? "

Answer : *" It was known from the very start that it was not the same "*

There was the cat out of the bag ! Only his Lordship failed to put the obviously proper question to follow :—

"Tell me, then, upon what element of suspicion you obtained the warrant of apprehension ? "

[This unasked but vital question we shall answer presently]

The brooch clue broke down on Saturday, 26th December, as early as 10 a m On the same day, nevertheless, at 2 p m , the police circulated among officers and constables a document, of which the following is an extract :—

"Wanted for identification for the murder at Queen's Terrace on 28th inst., Oscar Slater, sometimes takes the name of Anderson, a German, thirty-eight years of age ; 5 feet 8 inches. stout, square-shouldered. . etc , etc."

Here is blundering with a vengeance ! At 10 a.m the clue of suspicion against Slater is slain, and at 2 p m. an official instruction is issued that the suspect is wanted for identification Note also the futility of asking their own officers to find Slater for identification when, by this time, they know he is in Liverpool and getting ready to sail for America. Why not, instead of wild-goose chasing in Glasgow, send a message to the Liverpool police to stop him and send him back ?

Following the receipt in Glasgow of the official information from New York that the brooch clue was worthless, there must have been sore heads among the authorities to determine future action. Should they abandon the case, grant Slater his rightful liberty, or still hold on to the Micawber clue of something turning up? To have thrown up the case was, of course, the legitimate course, and there are substantial grounds for ascertaining that, before the *Lusitania* had actually reached New York, the authorities had realised the blunder of their cabled message and were preparing the public for the " let down " of complete abandonment. This, we ascertain from the reports in the Press. On the day Slater arrived in New York when everybody was on the tiptoe of excitement regarding the arrest of the man with the pawn-ticket, a Glasgow newspaper came out with a cold douche for its readers. It was declared that the most likely thing to happen at New York was that the suspect would prove his *bona-fides* and there would be an end to the whole business. The cabled arrest of Slater was described as " the boldest stroke of the police so far." Somebody *in the know* had penned that paragraph !

Slater had proved his *bona-fides*, but the promised " end to the whole business " was not forthcoming. Now that the whole world was looking on, to have released their arrested man would have been to confess their blunders and induce some sneers at the inefficiency of Glasgow Criminal Investigation. But, if to proceed was the order, what were they to proceed on? The reason for the persistence of the Glasgow authorities still to go on has hitherto been a mystery, but the present writer believes he has solved that conundrum also. Recovery of a copy of an official document has at length lifted the veil of obscurity concerning the continuation of the proceedings at New York, and the answer is made to Lord Guthrie's unasked question why the police held on after the brooch clue had collapsed *

This second attempt to associate Slater with the murder consisted solely of the supposition that he fled from Glasgow to avoid arrest. This is ascertained definitely from the terms of the newly-discovered document (printed in full in the Appendix), dated 2nd January, 1909 (the day of Slater's arrest at New York) This document discloses that Mr. J N. Hart, Procurator Fiscal for Lanarkshire, applied for a warrant of search against the premises lately occupied in Glasgow by the prisoner now at New York. It

*In the appendix will be found an explanation how the false originating clue of the brooch was obscured at the time and in its place, as the cause of arrest, was substituted the clue of identification

is specifically stated that Slater at that date had already been officially charged with murder at the instance of this official, and the grounds therein stated were that he had *absconded*

Let us see what evidence was on hand to justify this official taking such a step Slater's movements on leaving Glasgow and after arriving in Liverpool had been thoroughly investigated, and their *bona-fides* and openness made manifest That duty had been efficiently discharged by the Liverpool police. Statements from a dozen witnesses in that city had been taken and transmitted to Glasgow All this information, however, it had been apparently determined should be dismissed Taking a glance forward as to what happened at the trial in Edinburgh upon this important question of flight, which formed a very serious part of the Crown case against Slater, it was there declared by Superintendent Ord that Slater had " covered up his tracks as far as he could " The Lord Advocate made this statement to the Jury (" He, knowing that the police were on his track, took every step possible to baffle the ends of justice and to escape the hands of the authorities " To drive home to the Jury the appearance of flight, the Lord Advocate most erroneously declared that on the afternoon of 25th December, Slater's name and his full description were published in the

Glasgow papers, and that immediately he had begun his packing and later bolted

At the moment the Fiscal in his application for warrant declared that Slater had absconded, the authorities were in possession of the most complete information to the contrary We present to the reader an official statement which discloses precisely what was known We get this from the straightforward evidence of Superintendent Ord, furnished by him to the Commissioner at the 1914 inquiry.

"On the 23rd December he went down to Cook's office and inquired for berths in the *Lusitania* [This same witness declared at the trial · "I do not know that he was at Cook's office.*] He gave his name as Oscar Slater, and his address in Glasgow , he was offered two inside berths, but refused these on the ground that his wife was a bad sailor and he wished outside berths. It was suggested to him to take the inside berths and see if the agent would change them at Liverpool, and Cook's undertook to telegraph to Liverpool and he was to come back He afterwards called at the Cunard Company's offices and made inquiries there On the 25th Freedman and Hoppe (from London) called at Slater's house, and found him packing up."

*Page 105, ' Trial of Oscar Slater " in ' Famous Scots Trial Series "

[*Note* —This, it should be observed, omits
to say that Freedman and Hoppe had been
brought from London by Slater in pursuance of
an arrangement with them to take over the
house and furniture, and that morning Slater
had received from them a postcard intimating
their arrival.]

"He informed them that he intended to go
to Monte Carlo alone and leave the woman
behind Madame Freedman lent him £25
and then he agreed to take Madame Junio
with him. Thereafter he went down to the
railway station and hired a town-porter to
come to his house with a barrow He came
down about a quarter past eight, and Slater
gave him nine packages out at the door before
the neighbours. He left the house with his
two companions, he walking somewhat in
front. He arrived at the railway station
with them in a cab ; he found the town-
porter with his luggage and got him to
hand it over to a railway porter, who
labelled the luggage : ' Lime Street, Liverpool,' and paid the town-porter four
shillings.

"He then saw the excess clerk, who told
him to go and get his tickets, and he returned
with tickets which the excess clerk says
were for London. He informed the excess

clerk that he was going to Liverpool and paid the excess for that journey, and his baggage was put into the Liverpool van. He arrived in Liverpool and went to the North Western Hotel there He registered himself at the hotel as 'Oscar Slater, from Glasgow' In the morning he went along to the Cunard offices and saw Mr. Forsyth, whom he told he was staying at the North Western Hotel and that he wished berths on board the *Lusitania* He was offered two inside berths, and remarked that he had been offered these in Glasgow, and then seemed to check himself."

[In the original statement, taken from the Cunard Company's clerk by Sub-Inspector Bell, of Liverpool police, there is no mention whatever of this "seeming to check himself." Detective Bell declared that the clerk informed him that the man who called said "he was an American citizen and had just come from Glasgow and was staying at the North Western Hotel."]

"He got two outside berths, paying a little extra for them, and gave his name as Otto Sando He returned to his hotel and got his baggage handed over to a steamship porter He then went down to the steamer with the woman "

And that is what was described to the Jury as " covering up his tracks as far as he could " !

Mr Ord, it is to be added, after this very detailed statement as to Slater's movements, supplemented the same with this important declaration —

" That is *shortly* a fair summary of Slater's departure, so far as the police learned from all quarters *We passed on all this information to the Fiscal* "

Mr Ord seems here to have been washing his hands of the whole questionable affair As the matter stood, a mass of information establishing the openness of Slater's movements was unknown to the Jury in the final proceedings at Edinburgh, and the prisoner, in its absence, was represented to the Court as a fugitive who had taken every step to baffle the ends of justice by concealment of his identity and movements Mr. Ord, by his declaration, placed the responsibility upon the Fiscal for anything that had happened to the information which he had gathered and passed on to that official

It is clear, then, that when the Fiscal asked for his warrant of search upon the grounds of Slater having *absconded*, the information which the police had given him did not entitle him to do any such thing.

We have now arrived at a stage in the preparation of the case when we can definitely claim that two accusations made against Slater have completely broken down, and that it was pure folly for officials to persist with them —

(1) The Brooch clue and the erroneous cable to New York to hold up Slater on the pawn-ticket ,

(2) The charging of Slater as a murderer on the grounds of absconding

We are now to examine the third and worst blunder—that of alleged identification by eye-witnesses

THE EVIDENCE OF IDENTIFICATION

The public has heard much these days concerning the dangers of that class of evidence known as " identification ", This is the bringing against a prisoner of evidence by eye-witnesses speaking directly to the presence of a suspect at or near the scene of a crime, or running away from it. This class of evidence is deservedly in ill-repute ; it is the source of endless mistakes It was responsible for the Adolph Beck blunder, and there have been others only less notorious where innocent persons have been convicted and punished for crimes they did not commit. We do not propose to enter here upon a dissertation as to the dangers of that class of evidence The

Commission which sat on the Adolph Beck case declared it to be the worst of all classes of evidence, and that it was acceptable only under certain safeguards—particularly a pre-knowledge of the prisoner identified At the time of the Slater prosecution the Beck case was still fresh in the public and official mind, and the recommendations of the Commission ought to have been in the hands of every police department The Judge and Counsel in the Slater case, as a matter of fact, made allusion to the Commission's report. (We should have expected, at any rate, that the Glasgow authorities handling such a case as Slater's should have been well aware of these things, and endeavoured by the exercise of care and caution to prevent any repetition of the Beck blunders.) Let us see, however, to what use the Glasgow authorities put the recommendations of the Beck Commission in this early phase of the Slater case, while the prisoner is still in New York ?

All that was before them at that time as guides to the identity of the murderer was a group of statements, each contradictory of the other. These witnesses were Adams, Lambie, Barrowman, Agnes Brown and Mrs Liddell As regards the value of Lambie as a witness, we get a startling disclosure from the report of the 1914 Commissioner.

D

Two detective officers, Gordon and Pyper, declared to the Commissioner that on the night of the murder they had interviewed the servant maid and had received from her a declaration—in Gordon's case, positively, in Pyper's case, probably—that *she would not be able to identify the man*

At that moment the Commissioner had before him the problem whether the servant on the night in question had actually accused another man (vide Trench's statement) These two officers came forward then with that deadly statement regarding Lambie's inability to identify. They did not probably perceive that in so doing they were nullifying the witness and adding another link to the chain of accusations against the prosecution in that at the trial they put into the box to swear against Slater a witness who had already confessed to them that she could not identify the murderer at all

The Commissioner did not comment upon the fact that if at the trial, when in the box, these officers had disclosed to the Court what they now said that Lambie had declared to them, the Court must inevitably have instructed the Jury that Lambie's evidence could not be accepted against Slater.

Further, if these officers at the proper time reported to their chiefs that statement of Lambie's as to her inability to identify, then the sending of this girl to New York to attempt the identification of Slater must be added to their blunders in the case.

What, then, was the general position as to the evidence available ? Lambie, as an eye-witness, by her own admission, was valueless and ought not to be used. Next, Adams This witness was indefinite. His attitude was fair He said he had only seen the man on " a passing glance " and would not swear definitely to hat, clothes, or identity. Then a fresh witness, Miss Brown. This school teacher spoke of a couple of men running away from the scene of the tragedy, but alas ! in a direction entirely opposite to that taken by the single man supposed to have been seen by Barrowman

These five witnesses spoke each in contradiction of the other as to the garments worn by the assailant To straighten out and simplify matters we place in juxtaposition the garments of the assailant as described by these eye-witnesses during a period of seventeen minutes :—

Time of Observation	Witness	Suspect's Apparel
6 55 p m	Mrs Liddell	Long brown tweed overcoat with peculiar hem, brown tweed cap
7 10 p m	Helen Lambie and Mr Adams	Light grey overcoat, dark cloth cap
7 10 p m	Mary Barrowman	Fawn-coloured waterproof, Donegal hat and brown boots

Time of Observation	Witness	Suspect's Apparel
7 12 p m	Agnes Brown	Navy blue overcoat, velvet collar no headgear, black boots

Such were the contradictions presented to the Glasgow authorities upon this vital question of garments said to have been worn by the assailant ! From this hotch-potch of colours and clothes they were set the task to educe whether or not these descriptions pointed to one man, and that this man was Oscar Slater. Were they to abandon the hunt or to stretch the facts so as to vamp up a case ? In a subsequent trial in London, when the man Starchfield was prosecuted for the alleged murder of his boy, contradictions turned up in the course of the trial, which were the merest bagatelle to this conglomeration of nonsense. And there the prosecutor, Mr. Bodkin, abandoned the proceedings, confessing, with the Judge's concurrence, that he could not overlook the contradictions in clothes and hats. That was supremely straightforward and commendable. But here, in this wretched Slater case, the authorities decided that this mass of irreconcilabilities justified them in believing that Oscar Slater was the man to whom each of the witnesses somehow or other referred. No one can say by what logic the final judgment to proceed was arrived at. We only know that the decision was taken In the selection of the actual witnesses to be sent to New York it is noteworthy that they held back the most hopeless of the irreconcil-abilities—the two ladies, Miss Brown and Mrs Liddell, the very two who were the most intelligent

That arrangement left Lambie, Adams and Barrowman These three it was decided should be sent to New York. The document which showed that Lambie and Adams spoke of a separate man from Barrowman was *not* sent.

It was one of the requisite preliminaries, in order to meet the demands of the American Court of Extradition, that affidavits should be sworn by each witness before departure This was done An affidavit was also taken and sent on behalf of Agnes Brown This witness spoke of a couple of men seen by her running from the scene of the crime One was described as wearing a grey coat, which was held at that time to be in support of the description of Lambie and Adams Her second man wore a blue Melton overcoat and velvet collar The authorities thought for certain that Miss Brown's man in the grey coat pointed to Slater and supported Lambie and Adams We may add here that when Slater came back to Glasgow, instead of choosing the man in the grey coat,

Miss Brown picked out Slater as the man in the blue Melton overcoat and velvet collar, and so still more complicated the hopeless tangle of coats and colours

In the taking of the affidavits another ugly feature arose. Helen Lambie declared on oath that she had not seen the assailant's face, and that if shown a photograph she could not have identified it She declared she did not know whether the man was clean-shaven, wore a moustache or whiskers. We rather suspect that at this stage Lambie was disinclined to go further and was virtually telling the authorities not to send her But even that hopelessly negative statement to identification did not depress the authorities They still had hopes that Slater would be identified

One very pertinent observation we must interpose here as to the secrecy which obtains within the police system Recall that in the case of the three witnesses sent to America there was the secret document declaring that they spoke of two separate men The veriest novice in criminal work must perceive that the production of that document at any of the judicial proceedings which followed must have killed the entire case against Slater No Judge would tolerate a prosecution which put into the box witnesses to prove orally what the police believed themselves these witnesses could not prove, having definitely committed themselves in a document to that conclusion. Such an act is offensive to all beliefs in the efficiency and justice of criminal procedure.

Here stands revealed a grave evil in the whole system of secret criminal investigation —the knowledge among the higher authorities that they may put forward facts and opinions in documents, and then ignore them It is proved that this secret document was sent to every police staff in Scotland. A copy of it, in one of its several forms, was later actually procured by Mr William Roughhead and published by him, as editor of the " Famous Scots Trial Series," in the volume relating to the Slater case, and that gentleman added the significant footnote· " This bill was issued to the police forces *only*."* Let us see how far the evil of this suppression carried the case in the end We print side by side the declaration in the police document, with the observations of the Judge to the Jury at the trial .—

Official police statement upon Barrowman s description †	Excerpt from Judge s charge to Jury
"This man may have some connection with the murder, but *he should not be confounded with the man seen to leave the house by the servant and Adams*"	"You will have no doubt that the man that Lambie and Adams saw leaving the house and the man that Barrowman, the message-girl, saw on the street coming out of the close was *the same man, and the murderer*'

*Italics not ours

†This document was issued White Paper, page 7

on 24th December, 1908, see

Here we have the Judge in a Scottish Tribunal declaring to a Jury what was contradicted by the contents of a secret document in existence in every police office in Scotland And yet, of its existence not a word was known to Judge or Jury. Secrecy, it is apparent, is the highest virtue in the police system, it is higher than Judge or Jury; it transcends the rights of prisoners, it may permit truth and justice to be flouted. For our part we regard it as deplorable that Lord Guthrie was dispossessed of information to which every detective officer or constable in Scotland had access The one man, too, in the whole of the police services who had the courage to expose its existence, Lieutenant Trench, was dismissed from the Glasgow force by the Magistrates of the city on the ground that he had conveyed information* to others than in the police service Here the Magistrates of Glasgow involved themselves likewise in this pernicious gospel that Truth and Justice may be subordinate to the inviolate law of secrecy in the police establishments.

PROCEEDINGS IN NEW YORK

Let us now examine in detail the proceedings in New York.

At last, after sore perplexities, the Glasgow authorities have taken the plunge Oscar

*See official minute " Oscar Slater Trial " page 306

Slater is to be extradited from America and brought back to Scotland, the necessary preliminary to which is the setting up in a New York tribunal of a *prima facie* case that the prisoner was the murderer in Glasgow. Lambie, Adams and Barrowman are sent thither on the chance that somehow, anyhow, the irreconcilabilities of the descriptions of the assailant shall, in the actual presence of Slater, disappear and coalesce into an agreement that this is "*the man*." In brief, it was thought possible to show in New York that the prisoner in custody with the pawn-ticket in his pocket for his own brooch, the quick-change artist who had disported four overcoats in seventeen minutes, the philosophical fugitive who had cloaked his movements as openly as the advertised itinerary of a Cook's tour, would in his person reconcile all contradictions in descriptions and movements To profess to see a way through such a thicket of inconsistencies was to display a detective genius that made novices of all the creations of romance.

Everything now turns upon the case against Slater All else is subordinated, superseded, abandoned. Everything is thrown overboard concerning the investigation of the real problems of the tragedy—the mystery of the assailant finding his way into the house so quickly and

without alarming the occupant , the amazing
daring and savagery of the attack , the refusal
of the murderer to leave before he had put the
victim beyond the capacity of utterance and had
searched the private papers, to the neglect of so
much valuable jewellery , the strange matchbox found in the bedroom , the enigma of the
assailant escaping bloodstains while the scene
of the deed was so profusely marked , and, above
all, the police admission that the assailant was
probably known to the deceased*—all these vital
factors, pointing to a single deduction, were
thrown overboard and were heard of no more.
Everything in the way of investigation was now
converted into the finding of something that
would connect the elusive man in New York
directly or hypothetically with the crime. We
shall see presently into what perplexities this
erroneous method of conducting criminal investigation further brought the authorities

And now we turn to the happenings in New
York in support of their application to have this
man extradited and handed over to their officers
for return to Scotland ' Helen Lambie and Mary
Barrowman occupied the same berth on the
steamship to New York It was January, and
the voyage was protracted till the twelfth day

*As stated in the Glasgow newspapers, see page 66 for excerpt
from ' Glasgow Herald," of 26th December, 1908

These girls afterwards declared in Court that, although thus thrown together all the way, they had never exchanged a solitary word concerning the crime which had been the means of taking them this long journey—a silence irreconcilable with the mentality of such youthful females. When they came to make their appearance in the Court of Extradition at New York it was found that Helen Lambie, the servant-girl, whose affidavit had declared her to be ignorant whether the man had worn whiskers, moustache, or was clean-shaven, because she had not observed his face, had now departed from her original description. The garments worn by the assailant, as observed by her, had been subjected to some serious tailoring alterations. She was now and henceforth to the end of the case silent upon the light grey coat. She now expressed herself in complete accord with the fawn waterproof coat spoken of by Mary Barrowman. (Mr Adams, let it be said, was left alone to speak to the grey coat, and this gentleman never departed from his description, nor would he say that Oscar Slater was " the man ")

Before the opening of the official proceedings there arose that eternal bugbear of identification—the exhibition of a photograph or print of the man to be shown to the witness. This is a most improper act, much too common in police work.

After the Beck case the Chief of the Metropolitan
Police issued an instruction to his staff that
photographs were on no account to be exhibited
to witnesses to whom a prisoner was to be
shown. A very proper regulation, which might
have been copied to good advantage by other
Police Chiefs ! Here, in this Slater case, this
wise regulation was not observed One might
interpolate with an example in the writer's
experience of the dangers of this practice of
exhibiting photographs to witnesses It occurred
at a sitting of the High Court in Glasgow A
witness had identified one of three accused
persons in the dock. Counsel for defence asked
the witness what had caused him to particularly
remember this prisoner The answer was :
" His high cheek-bones " Having glanced
momentarily at the prisoner, Counsel turned to
the witness and asked whether he thought the
accused had higher cheek-bones than any other
person in the Court. To the utter dumbfounding
of everyone, the witness replied : '' Well, he had
high cheek-bones in the photograph the police
showed me ! "

It will be more appropriate in describing what
happened at New York to quote from the official
note of the proceedings. Counsel is cross-
examining the witness, Mary Barrowman. She
had admitted having been shown a photograph

of Oscar Slater in the office of Mr Fox, agent for the Glasgow authorities

Question · " When you went down to the Court were you looking for a man who was like the photograph ? "

Answer : " Yes "

Lambie, it may be interposed, refused to look at the photograph. She said she would not have known from a photograph

A still more serious irregularity in procedure was exposed by this question put to Mr Adams

" Were you present in the Court here when the girl Barrowman and the girl Lambie made their statements ? "

Answer : " Yes."

Question " And, of course, both Lambie and Barrowman had indicated that Slater was very like the man before you went on the witness-stand to give your statement ? "

Answer : " Yes "

Question " And you knew precisely where the man was sitting when you gave evidence ? "

Answer · " Yes, I admit that."

(The public will appraise the value of these alleged identifications.)

One may be pardoned for a still further digression We have seen how Adams admitted that he knew where Slater was seated and that Lambie and Barrowman, before him, had pointed out Slater.) Come now to the actual trial at Edinburgh four months later' The Lord Advocate is addressing the Jury, asking from them a verdict of "Guilty '"

Here is how this learned gentleman, the Highest Crown Official in Scotland, represented to the Jury the above incidents regarding the identification by Mr Adams of the prisoner at New York ·—

"When he [Mr. Adams] was taken to New York he identified him He was taken to a room where there were upwards of forty men and he had no difficulty whatever in picking this man out as being very like the man he had seen that night Never for a moment did he flinch He picked out that man as the only man that was like, or, as he said, the man he had seen that night "

The Lord Advocate further declared to the Jury "And Mr Adams says the prisoner *was the man.*" We quote again from the official evidence, Mr Adams speaking . " I pointed out Slater, but I did not say he was the man , I said he closely resembled the man "

The distinction between a witness affirming absolutely that a prisoner is " *the man* " and the reservation " *like the man* " is the difference between a verdict of guilty by the Jury, with the death sentence from the Judge, and, on the other hand, a verdict of acquittal   Life and death are involved in the two expressions   The prosecuting Counsel affirmed the former, the witness held to the latter

The real essence of the proceedings at New York, however, came to turn upon an incident which to the lay mind would have been considered unworthy of the dignity of consideration by a legal tribunal   As Oscar Slater was coming along the corridor to enter the Court accompanied by two men, unmistakably officers of Court, it was declared that both girls, Lambie and Barrowman, had pointed out Slater as the man they had observed at the murder. These girls seemed to have entered into a sort of competition which should claim to have been first in the identification   Barrowman declared she was first, saying   " ' There's the man coming ' before I heard Lambie say anything about it." Lambie, on the other hand, explained · " I was the first to identify him. I said ' There's the man coming,' and Mary Barrowman said ' Oh, ay, that's him ' ' "* What they clearly meant was—" This is the man whose photograph we have seen."

Although she had been silent hitherto upon any peculiarity of walk, Lambie now declared that

*Detective Pyper stated at the trial both identified the prisoner simultaneously

she identified Slater by such   In the Court when giving evidence Lambie failed to convey either by words or practical demonstration any understandable idea of the peculiarity   Finally, in cross-examination, matters were crystallized into this position :—

Question : " And the only thing that you can identify the man is by some manner of a walk that you cannot tell is different from any other man ? "

Answer : " Yes, that is a fact."

Lambie declared throughout the proceedings in New York that she did not see the man's face : it was the walk. She had, of course, before leaving Glasgow sworn she did not see the face and could not have identified a photograph if shown to her.

Mark the transformation in this girl's evidence when she came to the official murder trial at Edinburgh ! Here the final act in the burlesque of evidence was consummated   The witness now abandoned the walking peculiarity which in New York had baffled representation by her in words or acts   She now professed to say that she did observe the side of the man's face. We summarise the varying attitudes on her part towards the identification of the prisoner :—

(1) Her affidavit : Never saw the face.

(2) At New York (her own words) · " I saw
   the walk , it is not the face I went
   by, but the walk."

(3) At Edinburgh   " I am going on his
   face now "   (Her own words also)

Still further to destroy any value to be attached
to her statements   when a fawn waterproof coat
borrowed for the proceedings in the Court was
held up to her, she naively answered · " That's
the very coat he wore on the night of the
murder " The Judge afterwards observed to
the Jury that obviously she was a witness of mean
intelligence. His Lordship might have gone
further : " Gentlemen, you cannot hang a man
on sorry stuff of this sort !'

PREPARING A CASE

Slater, as earlier indicated, withdrew from the
proceedings at New York and came back voluntarily to Scotland to stand his trial. (He was
brought thither in mid-February) From the
moment of the prisoner's arrival the serious work
of preparing the case began to go forward.
Before the prosecution could face a Court, however, a long list of important points required to
be examined and fitted into the circumstances of
the prisoner, his belongings, his movements, etc)
In murder cases where investigations have been
properly conducted and definite grounds of guilt
ascertained before the charge is preferred, there

is always in the hands of the authorities, as the foundation of their prosecution, some major clue something which in itself is sound and solid enough to go to trial upon Minor clues as detected are added as supports. Here in the case under review the major clues were absent The inaugural clue of the brooch was dead · next that of " absconding " was, or ought to have been, buried along with it , identification, the most important of all, had not yet been seriously undertaken, for not much good had come of the American attempt to identify Slater. The performances of the two witnesses, Lambie and Barrowman, were not encouraging. Mr. Adams, refusing always to swear, did not help materially The " case," as it stood, was entirely hopeless for presentation to a Court. The prosecution had, then, to begin to look for a number of other items which mysteriously would be found to fit in with the charge against the prisoner

The following is a suggested list of the un-examined items of evidence which the Glasgow authorities were obliged to find as applicable to their prisoner, and once more marvellously they succeeded, or thought they did Such an enter-prise might be paralleled with a crew of fishermen who, before going to sea, nominate their catch and succeed, too, in returning with it !

(1) That the eye-witnesses, Lambie, Barrowman and Adams, would identify
Slater, notwithstanding the obvious
discrepancies in their statements and
the police document that there were
two men spoken of.

(2) That a number of witnesses, to be found,
would say they had observed Slater
loitering near the scene of the murder.

(3) That a weapon would be found among
Slater's belongings, which could be
held to account for the terrible
injuries inflicted upon the victim.

(4) That bloodstains might be discovered on
his wearing apparel.

(5) That they would prove that he fled out
of Glasgow, notwithstanding that the
Liverpool police had furnished abun-
dant information establishing the
bona-fides and unconcealment of the
movements of the prisoner.

(6) That apparel corresponding to that
spoken to by eye-witnesses would be
discovered among Slater's trunks.

The reader should never permit it to escape
his mind that these things were to be done
because this man, Oscar Slater, happened to
have exposed for sale in Glasgow a pawn-ticket
for a diamond brooch, which was his own
property.

The Authorities began straightaway on their quest for the new clues against the prisoner. On the day of his arrival Slater was " presented " A number of witnesses, speaking to the assailant running away from the house of the victim or to someone loitering in the vicinity of Miss Gilchrist's house, on dates prior to the occurrence of the tragedy, were brought to the Central police office, where the prisoner was on official exhibition amongst a row of men   This group consisted mainly of police officers in plain clothes and one or two railway officials. For the rightful preservation of the prisoner's interests, these arrangements were most unsatisfactory. To expect a row of Glasgow constables and railwaymen to offer "cover" to the identification of a German Jew, of unmistakable foreign appearance, was very much, as someone said, like attempting to conceal a bull-dog among ladies' poodles.   These proceedings were condemned by the distinguished expert, Sir Herbert Stephen, as a disgrace to a civilized country   By this he meant that Slater was deprived of the safeguards to innocence with which such proceedings are supposed to be invested

Supporting this declaration of Sir Herbert there are a number of remarkable evidences   Witnesses brought forward at the trial   to establish the loitering of the prisoner in the vicinity of

Miss Gilchrist's house prior to the crime, when under cross-examination as to the nature of the identification proceedings at the police office, frankly declared the prisoner to be " the only foreigner " in the group exhibited to them This admission exerted a twofold consequence It demonstrated that Slater had not been adequately safeguarded by the arrangements for identification.   Still more important, however, it proved that when, beyond all shadow of doubt, it was really Slater whom they had under observation, they distinguished him at once as a foreigner. Why, on the contrary, when they were observing the watcher in West Princes Street, did he fail to appear to them as a foreigner ? One of these witnesses, at whose door the watcher knocked and engaged in conversation with her, and who claimed to have identified him as Slater, declared at the trial, that she neither observed him to be a foreigner in appearance nor to speak with a foreign accent Note, now, the following remarkable contrasts ! The English witnesses who saw Slater on arrival at Liverpool, before he had become a murder suspect, uniformly declared in their statements to the Liverpool police that he spoke with foreign accent) and although it was the earliest hours of a December morning, one at least picked him out as a foreigner " a Dane," he thought   In Glasgow, the same clear-cut differentiation of him as a foreigner was made by every witness speaking to Slater in the flesh   Two girls who dealt with his laundry materials and who had only very casually met him, described him to the police correctly as "a German Jew"   Allan McLean, the man who reported him for exposure of the pawn-ticket, and who knew him only as a Mr "Oscar," used the same description "a German Jew"   The clerk in Messrs Cook's offices, Glasgow, who saw him briefly on two occasions, described him as "a foreigner"   The experienced Lieut Trench declared him at the trial to be "an obvious foreigner" and that no one who had seen the photograph of him published in the Glasgow newspapers could have failed to single him out at the official identification proceedings   What was the "description" furnished by the vital witnesses at the trial who were supposed actually to have seen the murderer before or after the crime ?   Of these principal witnesses, Lambie, Adams, Barrowman, Brown and Liddell, not a soul of them, at any time whatsoever, made the slightest allusion to this unmistakable feature, the obvious foreign appearance of their man.

On this material circumstance, so conspicuous as to be noticed by everyone who came in con-

tact with Slater, not one of those Glasgow witnesses came up to the scratch This single fact,
the omission by the Glasgow witnesses to draw
attention to the foreign appearance of their
man threw the whole of their evidence into a
position of weakness and unreliability, and,
considering the very pertinent and proper
objections to the methods of identification,
would have entitled a jury to have voted its
rejection in toto Of the other eye-witnesses
besides the New York group (Adams, Lambie
and Barrowman), Miss Agnes Brown, a school-
mistress, gave the police rather a rude shock
This witness came into the case because she
had read in the ' Glasgow Herald " a description
(provided by Lambie and Adams) of the man
seen to leave the house of the victim, in which
it was stated that he had worn a grey overcoat
Miss Brown's personal experience was this
She had, in walking along the street, encountered two men running away apparently from
the scene of the crime   One was dressed in a
grey coat , the second in a blue melton overcoat with velvet collar Accordingly it was
her view that the man in the grey coat whom
she had observed—and in this the police believed
she was supporting the evidence of Lambie and
Adams—would be the murderer But alas !
when she came to be confronted with Slater

at the identification proceedings, she picked him out, without hesitation not, however, as the man in the grey coat, but as the fellow in the blue melton overcoat) Moreover the two men whom she had observed were running away from the scene in a direction entirely opposite to the single man observed in flight by the message-girl Barrowman Miss Brown really destroyed the whole case for the prosecution) She made it impossible, if her evidence was accepted, for Lambie and Adams to speak to the man in the grey coat, and she made it impossible for Barrowman to testify to the man seen in flight along West Princes Street. (We shall see later how the authorities got round the corner of these perplexing difficulties! Then as regards Mrs. Liddell, the lady who saw the man waiting outside the house of the victim five minutes before the commission of the crime, she also, after much hesitation, picked out Slater, but she expressed her astonishment that the pale, sickly and ill-looking man whom she had observed on the night of 21st December, had, as the result of two months' bitter experiences in gaol, thrived so prosperously and become the hugely robust and hale man now presented to her.) Let it be said also there was another solid objection to this lady's evidence She had not made any statement either to the police or her own people concerning the man whom she had observed in wait at Miss Gilchrist s house until forty-eight hours after the occurrence of the tragedy, and this notwithstanding that she had been rudely acquainted with the horrors of the crime within one minute of its happening, and had actually heard the sounds of the murderer in the brutal act of killing.

Then there were the above-mentioned people brought to see Slater, who thought they had observed a man loitering in West Princes Street near to Miss Gilchrist's abode at dates prior to the happening of the crime   None of them had beforehand spoken of any such man, or had reported his presence to the constable on street patrol   Here we enter upon the most dangerous class of evidence responsible for such painful blunders as happened in the Adolph Beck case, where an innocent man was twice erroneously convicted by evidence picked up from the streets. Ordinary human nature is scarcely to be trusted in this terribly serious business of certifying to a man, of whose appearance they have only the most casual knowledge and who happens to be associated with a charge of murder   On this point, the actual eye-witness, Mr. Adams, who undoubtedly saw the murderer pass out of the house, adopted the proper attitude. He declared always : " I only got a passing glance.

I say he is like the man, but I will not swear
he is the man " That is the legitimate and
correct standpoint for all witnesses of this class
speaking to someone observed during a brief
transitory moment) They ought only to be
positive in respect of their being possessed of
previous knowledge of the prisoner or from
some unmistakable feature pointed out by
them and seen by Judge and Jury to be a positive
reality.

Let us momentarily examine some of the
stuff that did actually pretend to identify Slater
at these proceedings and was accepted by the
Crown and produced against Slater at the trial.
One man, speaking not to the prisoner but to the
dozen other men, the policemen among whom
he was ranged, thus described their appearance
at the trial " They were not policemen , I
think they were all small persons I saw various
types of sallow complexions, black moustaches
and *broken noses* " A "Cruikshanks" caricature
of Glasgow's noble force ! Another witness
declared that at first she wasn't sure of Slater,
but had been thinking it over, and was *now* sure
A third professed to identify him by his *back*,
seen at a distance of thirteen yards on a December
night. A fourth was proved to be entirely in
error in testifying that he had observed Slater
on a Sunday evening prowling in West Princes

Street, while the prisoner showed by independent witnesses that he had never left his own home on the night in question   In a chapter following relating to Slater's alibi it will be shown that still another witness who spoke against the accused, basing her identification on this con- demned " passing glance " opportunity, was *completely wide of the mark and in proven error*   This witness, moreover, confessed, as also did others, that before going in to identify Slater she had been shown his photograph and description—a grave impropriety indeed

A motley collection of stuff of this sort, dignified with the label " evidence," was accepted by the authorities and used at the trial to support their preconceived theory that Slater for nearly two months preceding the tragedy had watched the house of Miss Gilchrist in West Princes Street. Slater arrived n Glasgow from London just two months prior to the murder, and accordingly must have straightway proceeded upon his daily vigils It is an inconceivable assumption. No one was able to say that Slater had ever heard of the deceased (see his own story in the appendix where he declared he had never even heard the name of the victim) In a document, published page 86, the police had committed themselves definitely to the view that they did not know how he had come to hear of the old lady having jewellery in her possession and hazarded the speculation to account for it by declaring that " he might have come to hear of Miss Gilchrist having jewels through the bookmakers in the Sloper Club " That was a confession of complete ignorance, a mere blind guess Yet we have the same officials who prepared that document attempting before the Jury by this weak class of evidence to establish that the prisoner had been in daily observation of Miss Gilchrist's house almost from the hour of his coming to the city. The whole of this " Loiterers' " evidence we should have no hesitation in dismissing as worthless, nay, dangerous. It was obtained by solicitation, and it had for its origin that apparently ineradicable assumption in the police mind that burglary was the indisputable motive of the crime It was simply another exhibition of that common fatality in human nature, the authorship of all wrongeous convictions, to see in innocent circumstances actual relationship with a crime which is beforehand deep in the minds of the witnesses

It was long ago pointed out by Voltaire in circumstances of a similar character in connection with a murder for which an innocent man, Jean Calas, had been convicted and broken on the wheel, that a large volume of evidence coming before a Court is apt to sway its judgment, not

because of its truth but because of its multiplicity
Voltaire laid it down as an excellent guide that
the proper test for evidence of this sort was to
disregard the multiplicity and to seek to apply
to the circumstances of the crime the real significance of the utterances of the witnesses. Apply
this test to the Slater case ! Despite the array
of evidence of the " broken-nosed " policeman
variety, it is conclusive in fact that the prisoner
did not watch the house of Miss Gilchrist. Suppose
we concede that he did.   After his many weeks'
patient vigil what was the result as applied to
his ultimate acts ? Of the many opportunities
available to him for putting into execution the
accrued advantages of his observations, he
chose precisely the very worst. He blundered
into the house during a ten-minutes' absence of
the servant-maid and when, to get out again, if
he intended to remain long enough to collect the
hoard of jewellery, he would most probably have
had to commit, not a single but a double murder
—the returning servant-maid as well as her
mistress   This ugly difficulty for the prosecution was perceived by the Judge at the trial
Lord Guthrie declared that there seemed to be
two murders within the scope of the assailant's
calculations. That is not what one would
expect from a burglar accredited with two
months' vigil of the house. As a matter of fact,

* Instructive to follow an untenable premise to its
logical conclusion.

on two afternoons of the week, Sundays and Thursdays, the maid was granted a long absence, while on the afternoon of the very day on which the crime was committed he could have had several hours' freedom from the presence of the maid, who had gone out on a message which needed this lengthy absence   It is an absolute postulate of any belief in a lengthened watching of the movements of the inmates of the house that the assailant would have entered only when he had the old lady herself to be dealt with, and the maid absent for such a period as would allow him an uninterrupted exit   Why the actual assailant entered the house during that brief and dangerous ten minutes' absence of the maid is a mystery which can only be explained by the theory of the murder advanced by the late Lieutenant Trench, which will be found in a later chapter

THE WEAPON

Considering the mists of uncertainty surrounding so much else in their hands, it was indispensable to the prosecution to bring home to the prisoner the possession of an instrument which would either show bloodstains upon it or be held by experts to have been capable of inflicting such deadly injuries as appeared upon the deceased. A small tin-tack hammer of Woolworth magnitude had been found in one

of the trunks brought back from America as
Slater's property   These had been seized and
sealed at the moment of his arrest in New York ,
and had been under the constant eye and care
of the Glasgow officials who were sent to escort
the prisoner back to Glasgow.   These trunks, let
it be said (and of this not a word was allowed to
emerge at the trial, although testified to by
Detectives Trench and Cameron) disclosed pains-
taking and methodical packing   Between the
layers of their contents there had been inserted
pieces of camphor—the clearest evidence that
the owner, when packing, had neither been
flurried nor hurried, as the Lord Advocate so
vigorously made out before the Jury   Lieutenant Trench gave it to the writer as his opinion that
several days must have been spent in the laborious
process of packing the nine trunks

On their being opened at Glasgow, attention
was at once directed to the presence of the
hammer   It was instantly pounced upon as
the instrument that might suit the purpose of
the authorities in taxing Slater with the possession of a weapon to be associated with the crime
Here we might interpose with the observation
that to ascribe to a burglar and murderer the
idiocy of taking his weapon to New York in his
own trunks was equivalent only in futility of
judgment to the earlier police blunder of con-

sidering that Slater had run round Glasgow asking strangers to purchase from him a pawn-ticket for a diamond brooch, when all Glasgow was aflame with the hue and cry for a brooch or pawn-ticket. Since the conviction of Slater, Sir Herbert Stephen has undertaken the task of examining the records of every murder in which a hammer was used as the weapon , and in every case he discovered that the murderer had thrown it away. Besides, this was not an isolated implement in Slater's trunks He had purchased the hammer on a cheap 2s 6d. card of household tools , and the entire card, not the the hammer alone, was packed in his trunks. These points were not disclosed to the Jury

However, the authorities set out to get at Slater on the question of the hammer The first step was to hand it over to Professor Glaister, of Glasgow University, to report upon, whether its surfaces showed signs of blood or answered, in its use, to the character of the injuries found upon the deceased. The Professor had made an earlier report in similar fashion upon the likelihood of an old auger, which had been discovered in the yard to the rear of Miss Gilchrist's house, in which was stated " on examination we found that adhering to the metal of the instrument were several grey hairs and what seemed to be blood " The conclusive test,

auger

chemical analysis, disclosed the supposed blood to be rust spots, and the auger was found to have been thrown out of an adjacent workshop and had nothing whatever to do with the murder

Professor Glaister gave it as his opinion in Court that there was no weapon in the dining-room to account for the wounds on the deceased He expressed the view that the assailant could have killed Miss Gilchrist with the hammer, employing it from twenty to forty times—one witness said from forty to sixty times—and, further, that he could not have escaped receiving a considerable share of blood An overcoat found in Slater's trunks—the garment he had worn during the four days he remained in Glasgow after the crime—was also subjected to examination by skilled witnesses, but neither upon it nor the hammer were blood-stains found The authorities then put forward the assumption that the coat and hammer had been washed. Dr Adams could have told the Jury that, in his opinion, a chair and not the hammer was the instrument of death; but his evidence was not heard Superintendent Douglas, with Lambie and Adams, could have told them that, so far as they could see, there were no stains upon the murderer's clothes when he left the house; nor had he washed the coat. In putting forward the theory, therefore, that the coat might have been washed to rid it of supposed guilty bloodstains, the authorities were going beyond the actual facts ascertained by themselves in their earliest investigations (It is known, too, that the police searched the house vacated by Slater on his departure, and found there not a solitary vestige of incriminating evidence, yet here, in the production of the coat and hammer, and in their attack upon these articles, the authorities were going upon the inconceivable assumption that Slater had packed into his trunks and conveyed to America the only possible material clues to his guilt that were to be found

It was observed, too, when the hammer was being impressed upon the Jury as the weapon of the crime, that the violence of the noises which had so much alarmed the Adams family was now considerably subdued (Mr Adams had told Lambie when he encountered her at the door of the victim on the night of the murder " there was a terrible knocking in your house, the ceiling was like to crack ") At the trial, when the hammer and not the chair was alleged as the weapon, the noises were described as " not heavy noises " A tin-tack, 8-oz hammer could not have cracked a ceiling

The Contradictions of Mary Barrowman

During some period of this preparatory stage, when the authorities were getting ready their case for the trial by taking the official precognitions of the several witnesses whom they intended to put forward as evidence, there arose in connection with the statements of Mary Barrowman, a problem of a most extraordinary kind, which, when it came to light, must have struck consternation in the minds of those responsible for the further proceedings. Knowledge of this is due to the exposures by Lieutenant Trench. Comment upon it here is all the more indispensable since from the attitude towards it of the Commissioner who sat at the 1914 inquiry, it is manifest that officialdom desires it to be hushed up. It is perhaps the most serious of the many strange things done in this wretched case, and it is precisely here where the attempt to draw an explanation has been met by guarded official reticence.

This little message-girl was the solitary witness at the trial who was positive in her identification of Slater as " the man " whom she had observed on the night of the murder run from the scene along West Princes Street. Her positive evidence it was that turned the scales against Slater. After her return from New York,

when officially called upon to renew her statement of evidence, already written down and
sworn to on oath, she must have made it known
that she was departing from what she had said
concerning her own movements on the night in
question) This girl must have made a confession to the official who was taking her evidence
at this later date that what had been sworn to
earlier was incorrect, and that she now was
wishful to depart from it. The girl had first
declared that after eight o'clock, or just one
hour later to her alleged encounter with the
assailant, as he reached the street from the stairway at the victim's house, she had gone to a
brother's shop and in so doing had, a second
time, passed through West Princes Street. On
this second occasion she saw the crowds assembled
in front of the victim's house ; was told of the
murder and then thought of the man in flight
who might have had something to do with the
crime.   In our earlier reference to this witness
we pointed out that she kept all this information
to herself and did not speak until her mother
two days later had thrust her into the case ; the
mother, confessing, too, at the trial that she
thought it was only a " story."

This part of her statement she now entirely
contradicted and wished to be deleted. She
asked to have substituted a statement that she

had, after 8 p m., attended a Band of Hope meeting near Maryhill (a direction disagreeing entirely with that of her first statement) and had there learned through someone coming into the meeting of the occurrence of a murder in the city. In company with other girls she had later gone to West Princes Street, saw the crowds assembled at the place where she had earlier observed the man emerge, etc , etc

Here was a serious problem for the officials ! Their principal witness was now disclosing to them a vital departure from an earlier declaration on oath. Incidentally, this after-New York alteration in evidence proved that the authorities had sent her to America without having checked the authenticity of her statement There was the story of this girl having gone to her brother's shop, and no officer had been despatched thither to check the witness's statement, while regarding her actual presence at the scene of the murder there was the strange feature that Adams and his sisters and Lambie, who were all on the street within a minute of the man's emergence from Miss Gilchrist's house, were unanimous in declaring that no one was to be seen   That there was some flutter in the official dovecots over this remarkable development is apparent from the statement of Detective Pyper before the 1914 Commissioner to the effect that in

February, 1909, he had gone back to Barrow-man's employer for another precognition as to his employee's movements. It was strange that this employer was not produced at the trial; and there is this further inexplicable omission to record on the part of the Commissioner that Detective Pyper produced to him the document containing the statement made by the employer as to Barrowman's movements and this the Commissioner failed to include in his report We get only a glimpse of its contents in the published report. "Subsequently, in February 1909, I took a precognition from him (the employer), *which is now produced*, from which it appears that he had no recollection of her being sent on the message and there was no entry in the book of cash transactions and nothing to show where they sent goods on 21st December "

This departure by Barrowman from her sworn statement was one of the matters which was placed before the Commissioner of 1914 for his investigation. Lest any mistake or oversight should occur in regard to a matter of such serious importance the Glasgow Solicitor, acting for Lieutenant Trench, wrote to the Commissioner desiring him, when the witness Barrowman was before him (in his secret room) to put to her the discrepancies in her two statements and to call for her explanation   The law agent further made a direct charge against the witness (the serious terms of it are published in the White Paper of 1914)   He declared that this witness had either lied at the trial or lied in her first statement

And what transpired when this challenged witness was taken before the Commissioner ?

Nothing , absolutely nothing '

It is almost incredible that this legal gentleman in such a situation overlooked entirely the challenge by the Law Agent and Lieutenant Trench   In his Shrieval capacity the Commissioner was in the habit of swearing witnesses before Almighty God to speak the truth, the whole truth, and nothing but the truth   Here he permitted the girl when she came before him to renew precisely the statement as she had made it to the Jury , and completely ignored the serious discrepancy it offered with the earlier statement before Sheriff Glegg on oath   Not a word was mentioned that another statement had been made.   No unprejudiced mind can possibly reconcile this inexplicable action on the part of the Commissioner with a true appreciation of the facts of the case.

And this gentleman, having failed to put to her for explanation the glaring contradictions of the two statements, when submitting his report of the proceedings to the Secretary for Scotland, actually paid the witness the compliment that she seemed "to be honest and anxious to tell the truth." We make no accusation against her to the contrary, but if the report itself were true, then the Commissioner exposed himself to the criticism that it must have been he who prevented her speaking "the whole truth" regarding the two statements by her.

To make matters clear we append together the two conflicting statements

MARY BARROWMAN

Original Deposition	*Extract from Evidence at Trial*
'After leaving our shop at 8 p m I went to my brother s shop at 480 St Vincent Street and while going there I again passed along West Princes Street and saw a crowd opposite No 49 I learned of the murder and I then thought of the man I had seen running out of the close there	I had gone with my message and then back to my employer s shop and then to a Band of Hope meeting (this meeting in Landsdowne Mission Hall, Walker Street, Hopehill Road), there I heard of the murder and I went back to West Princes Street because of hearing of the murder I saw a number of people there ''
According to this statement she would learn of the murder about 8 15 p m	According to this statement she would learn of the murder about 10 p m

That the Commissioner had every opportunity of knowing the glaring weakness in the evidence of this witness, is apparent from this little excerpt from the evidence of Superintendent John Ord at the same inquiry :—

"I show the original statement made of Miss Mary Barrowman in which she says that after leaving the shop at 8 p m. she went to her brother's shop at 480 St Vincent Street   She does not mention going to the Band of Hope meeting, but that was only a statement made in a hurry but afterwards a more extended statement was got from her "

In this statement there is a suggestion that it was all just a matter of hurry , that the extension from the shorter to the longer statement made matters all right That will not do at all   Superintendent Ord himself, when giving evidence at the trial declared to the jury that he got the evidence of Barrowman "*in full*" on the morning of 24th December * Barrowman's first statement disclosed that she heard of the murder at 8 15 p m in West Princes Street, whereas she told the Jury she was informed of the murder in the Band of Hope meeting at Maryhill two miles away and arrived at the scene to re-hear of it from the crowds about 10 p m   The two statements can neither be reconciled in point of time nor place

Now let us see about the alleged hurry !

We get it from the evidence of Mrs Barrowman (the mother) at the trial that two detectives waited at her house a whole evening for Mary to come in and give her first statement.   Then

*See Page 122, Book of Trial

E1

we find that Detective Pyper next morning took
from her a further statement   Next she was
seen by the Fiscal (the highest Glasgow authority)
and then, finally, her statement was carefully
reduced to writing, read over to her before
Sheriff Glegg and she took an oath upon its
accuracy and signed it.*   Not much hurry or
liability to momentary error in all that ¹   The
very contrary indeed   It is most singular, too,
and only makes the confusion worse confounded,
that Mrs Barrowman, when in the witness-box
at the trial, informed the Jury that Mary had
said to her, when the detectives came to take
her first statement, she had been to a Band of
Hope meeting   Either the detectives or the
mother had heard badly   The Band of Hope
meeting was not revealed to the police until
mid-February, eight weeks after the first call of
the officers   Without imputing anything to the
witness, one can see that any mention in the
Court of the first statement, that she had gone
to the brother's shop, coming from the mother,
would have wrecked the evidence of the girl—
and wrecked the case along with it

This girl, it should be noticed, received from
the authorities £100 for the part alleged to have
been played by her in the arrest of Slater

*The other girl witness, Lambie declared at New York that
her statement before the Fiscal had been written and re-written
so many times she could not tell the number

A NEW WITNESS

One of the purposes of this publication is to make known the evidence of a party hitherto unheard of in the case who makes the claim that she was an eye-witness in West Princes Street on the night of the murder at the precise moment when the assailant rushed from the stairway at Miss Gilchrist's flat and reached the street, a party covering in her observation the time and place claimed by the girl Barrowman   This witness, a woman who at the time in question was engaged as a Restaurateur in Glasgow, managing four of those establishments, was prevented by circumstances, to be afterwards indicated, from giving her evidence at the trial for the defence   It is her statement that she saw the man run from the stairway at Miss Gilchrist's house, and that Oscar Slater positively was not that man. This lady is still alive and reaffirms to-day her declaration that Slater was not the man. This person at the time of the trial in Edinburgh adopted an attitude not uncommon with many people, undesirous to be mixed up with a murder case, and in holding to this decision to refrain from giving evidence was very much influenced by her husband who besought her to keep clear of law-courts. On publication in the press of Slater's photograph, after his return from New

York, this party declared that the man she
had encountered on the street running away from
the house of the victim did not at all resemble
these published photographs. However, when
the trial actually came round and the proceedings
daily received so much publicity, being dissatisfied with the statements made in Court by
witnesses to the identification of Slater as the
man seen to run from Miss Gilchrist's residence,
she decided to make a call at the offices of the
Glasgow Solicitors acting in the defence of the
prisoner. She visited the offices of Messrs
Shaughnessy, and explained the position. The
partner who saw her (he is still alive and confirms) was impressed with her statement, took it
down and sent a copy at once to Edinburgh for
the Court, the trial still being in process of
hearing. It was too late, however, the writer
understands, to do anything with the statement,
and the evidence was accordingly not forthcoming in Court for the defence, where its value
to Slater would have been enormous.

At a later date Mr Shaughnessy handed the
writer, in journalistic capacity, a copy of the
statement, and which is now printed in full in
the appendix as taken from the original. The
writer has recently traced the witness and
obtained from her confirmation of her original
statement and repeated also an expression of her

willingness to give evidence before any tribunal
that may be set up, the effect of which, as before
stated, is that Slater was not the man who was
seen to run from the house of the murdered
woman

Apart from the direct value to the defence which
this evidence affords its disclosure has this consequence that it cuts seriously into the testimony
of Mary Barrowman, the other eye-witness to
the flight of the assailant from the stairway
That evidence, as we have seen has already
suffered the detraction that, in respect of her
own movements on the night of the tragedy, she
was fundamentally in error in either her first
sworn statement or in her later evidence before
the Court This new witness, if we may so
speak of her, claims to have occupied on the
street at the moment when the fugitive appeared
from the stairway, a position precisely similar
to that claimed by Barrowman and each
declares there was no one else there Mary
Barrowman stated that after the man had
passed her she took it into her head to turn and
go after him for a distance of fifty yards or so,
before retracing her steps to proceed with her
message, which was to take a pair of repaired
shoes to a customer of her employer On a
wet, dirty December night that, surely, was a
strange act on the part of a message-girl By

way of explanation for its strangeness she tendered at the trial the excuse that she thought the man was running to catch a tramcar   For our present purpose, however, it is apparent she must have been detained at or near the spot for at least a minute or two ; and it is to be recalled that by this time Mr Adams, followed quickly by Lambie, and the two Miss Adams, were standing on the street   All of these people swore that there was no one else to be seen. The point about this new witness is that she claimed no detention at the spot.   After being knocked down by the assailant in flight she picked herself up and went on her way   We leave readers to study the problem for themselves, remembering that if the evidence of Mary Barrowman is to be rejected, the entire case against Slater goes by the board   Barrowman was the one positive witness to his identification

The police have all along made much of the fact that this witness pointed out from the first that the fugitive had a twisted nose, and insinuated that this corresponded with the Jewish nose of Oscar Slater   It completely knocks the bottom out of any pretended value to this detail that at New York, Barrowman blandly informed the Court that never before in all her life had she seen a man in Glasgow with a twisted nose   It is evident the Commis-

sioner did not swallow that extraordinary
statement, he turned to her and asked the
significant question "How old are you?"
Slater, let it be said, was not possessed of a
twisted nose Prisoners emerging from Peterhead prison have declared that this "twisted
nose" description led them entirely astray in
their attempts to locate Slater in the prison

MANIPULATION OF EVIDENCE

In its veneration for the efficiency and justice
of our criminal system, it is an assumption by
the public, never questioned, that the evidence
which emerges during the hearing of a great
murder trial, constitutes the sum-total that has
been ascertained of the crime and the association
with it or otherwise of the prisoner This con-
ception is rudely dispelled by the discoveries and
after-revelations in this notorious case since
the trial took place Here we are sharply confronted with the displeasing fact, shown in
earlier chapters, and now to be more fully
presented, that the evidence submitted to the
Court covered only part of the actually known
circumstances of the crime and the relation to it
of the person in the dock Granted there rests
upon the officials of the Crown, so as not to over-
load and unduly protract the proceedings, a duty
to sift, winnow and limit the evidence, but
here there was much of material importance to

the ascertainment of the truth that was rejected, while much in the hands of the police was unknown to the Defence that was material to the safety of the prisoner It is upon these aspects we are now to speak

On the first day in Glasgow when Slater was shown to witnesses for identification purposes the prosecution was faced with circumstances which were perhaps more destructive of their case than even the earlier discovery of the blunder of the brooch clue Prior to this, it should be mentioned, the police had been making inquiries into the movements of Slater on the night of the murder, collecting anything that seemed to cloak him in an atmosphere of suspicion Thus they had interrogated the German servant-girl, Catherine Schmalz, who had been in Slater's service up to the night of his departure and had been then dismissed This girl was in the hands of the police, accessible to them virtually from the hour of her dismissal Her evidence was accordingly purged from any influence or contamination by the suspect This witness was emphatic in her statement that Slater dined in his own house with Antoine and herself on the night in question, his dinner-hour corresponding with the hour of the tragedy, 7 p.m Slater, in his movements, had also been traced to a billiard room in Renfield Street, about a mile

away from the scene of the crime, at or near
the hour of 6 40 p m , when he left to go home
for dinner   As Sir Arthur Conan Doyle long
ago observed, this did not give him time to go to
his house to get the murderous hammer and be
on the spot at West Princes Street, to be seen
by Mrs Liddell at 6 55 p m , waiting for the
appearance of the maid   The mistress, Antoine,
also corroborated that Slater dined at home.
These ascertainments from witnesses cut seriously
into the Crown case   They gave to Slater the
nucleus of a substantial alibi.

On the day of identification under notice,
among the witnesses who were asked to the
Central Police Offices was one, Duncan McBrayne,
a Glasgow business man   He had known Slater
as a customer at his shop in Sauchiehall Street.
This gentleman had earlier gone to the police
and reported that on the night in question,
about the hour of 8 15, or just one hour after
the tragedy, he had observed Slater standing
quite unconcernedly at the entry to his own
residence   This was information disconcerting
to the prosecution   They had by this time
decided, by means of the evidence of a ticket
sales girl at Kelvinside Subway Station, to
prove that Slater at 7.35 p m , in a state of great
excitement, had entered the subway, been
whirled out to the suburbs of Glasgow and there

concealed himself, to return later in the evening and run to the Sloper Club " gasping and panting for money." The effect of this statement of McBrayne was to controvert and destroy this story of the subway McBrayne's statement brought Slater to his own door with no suspicion of alarm.

The authorities accordingly brought McBrayne to the Central Police Offices to see if it were really true in respect of his identification. McBrayne at once picked out Slater from the group as the man he had seen at Charing Cross at the moment he was supposed to have been in the subway Slater himself returned the recognition by saying " Oh, you're the man in the big shop in Sauchiehall Street!" Here the identification was mutual, conclusive and unassailable in its authenticity We make bold to say that, in respect of title to speak to identification, on the sure ground of pre-knowledge, McBrayne was worth a dozen of the other witnesses

Yet mark the sequel !

McBrayne declared further there was no possibility of his being under any misapprehension as to the night of his observation of Slater He explained that on the occasion under notice he had just closed his premises and was on his way home along Sauchiehall Street when he saw Slater About that time he had also noticed a passing ambulance wagon and, upon reading in the newspapers next morning of the tragedy, he immediately connected the ambulance with a journey to the scene of the murder That circumstance indelibly fixed in his mind the date of his observation of Slater This was an ugly snag for the prosecution Here, upon indisputable evidence, Slater is fixed at his own doorstep at 8.15 p m , and the girl at the subway station, a mere " passing glance " witness, shown to be entirely in error —innocently but still in error

And what was the police solution to the enigma ? McBrayne or the subway girl ? The subway girl—manifestly because she supported the idea of flight and alarm Against the utilisation of this witness there was another potent reason which was tossed aside She declared the fugitive to run down the steps of the subway station at 7 30 or 7 35 p m The murderer left the victim's house precisely at 7 10 and was seen at full speed at 7.12 dashing from the scene A detective officer declared at the trial he had walked the distance from Miss Gilchrist's to the subway in seven minutes Slater should have been there at 7.15 He could have crawled on hands and knees and arrived at the subway by 7 30. The Lord Advocate saw this difficulty and tried to explain it away to the Jury by saying that Slater must have doubled up and down all the side streets—a fugitive of a new kind indeed

The Lord Advocate, commenting generally upon the absence on the prisoner's part to produce to the Court evidence of his movements on the night of the tragedy made this condemnatory observation to the Jury " There is no man so destitute of friends and circumstances that he cannot establish his identity and show who he is and what he is and what his movements were and where he was at the time the crime was committed which is laid at his door."

Yes, we reply, how might he have fulfilled these demands upon himself made by the Crown when the action of the police had robbed him of the very friends who could have spoken to his movements and was thereby deliberately thrust into that state of " destitution " which was charged to his account ?

The absence of McBrayne, the soundest of all the witnesses to identification and his substitution by the girl* suggests to the writer something which struck at the very roots of justice , something against which the prisoner ought to have indisputable right of redress

*This girl, as did others, admitted that a photograph of Slater and his description had been shown to her

This business of McBrayne's suppression as a witness was another of the items brought to the attention of the 1914 Commissioner. That gentleman heard McBrayne, who repeated to him in full the statement   and that was an end of it also' Not a word of enquiry was instituted by the Commissioner at the authorities as to how such a valuable piece of evidence was kept back from the prisoner's defence   Nor was any comment offered upon the obvious deduction that McBrayne's evidence ruled out as an error the whole story of the prisoner rushing to the subway and concealing himself in the suburbs till a late hour

One point more about McBrayne. This party differed from the other witnesses. He had gone voluntarily to the police in the interests of justice for protection of the prisoner In this act there was laid upon the police the obligation, if they did not want his evidence, to send him to the agent for the prisoner McBrayne did not belong to the police, he belonged to justice.

McBrayne's evidence cut with a double-edged sword into the case for the prosecution and completed the alibi set up by the defence on the prisoner's behalf We are confronted also with this ugly fact that as the Prosecution preceded the Defence in the submission of its evidence at the trial, the authorities must have been pretty sure, when they went on with the subway girl's story, that McBrayne had not been discovered by the defence and was not to be a witness for Slater   That is a circumstance which makes his suppression almost a criminal act. McBrayne supported the alibi of the prisoner that he dined in his own home Antoine, Schmalz and McBrayne set up one connected link from 7 p m till 8 15 p.m proving Slater's disconnection with the crime. Slater's own statement as to the night in question (as furnished to his law agent while lying in prison in February, 1909, printed in the Appendix) was that he most likely went downstairs about 8 p.m and there McBrayne found him, whereas he was erroneously represented to the Jury as having fled to the suburbs, hid himself there, and returned later to a club " gasping and panting for money "

Nor did this exhaust all the omissions that combined to damage the prisoner's case. The authorities were in possession of complete details of Slater's open movements after he left Glasgow, as was earlier shown. This was, however, entirely cut out. Porters and others in Glasgow could have proved before his departure the labelling of his trunks " Lime Street, Liverpool." These trunks were actually in Court so labelled and were not shown to the Jury

(The writer a number of years ago saw one of them in the offices of Messrs Shaughnessy, Glasgow, and it still bore this label) A little interpolation may assist further in exhibiting the absolute honesty of the prisoner in the *bona-fides* of his movements) While in prison in Glasgow awaiting his trial, Slater informed his agent (taking his statement) that he had travelled to Liverpool that night in a through-carriage. This statement of the through-carriage was denied by railway officials The agent reported this to Slater in turn. The prisoner answered most defiantly that he did travel in such a carriage It was only after the agent's repeated interviews with the railway men that an official recollected that it was Christmas night and that a special through-carriage had been added to the train but for that night only.) The " fugitive from justice " corrected even the railway people

All the considerable volume of evidence discovered by the Liverpool police as to Slater's open movements in that city was ignored,) so also McBrayne's evidence, so also Doctor Adams speaking of the chair. The only part that was salved from this jettisoned evidence was the Cunard Company's clerk at Liverpool regarding whom there will be mention later (In absence of all this the prosecution declared that

Slater had covered up his tracks as far as possible so as to baffle the police

Further, at the trial itself, there was a renewal of this policy of choice of evidence The Crown may claim a right here, but we rather imagine the public will dispute it It was decided to leave out the evidence of the school teacher, Miss Agnes Brown This lady was actually in the witness room but was not called She was prepared to speak to Slater running away from the scene in a direction in entire disagreement with Barrowman, while the fugitive she had observed was wearing a blue melton overcoat with velvet collar As the Jury, in Mrs Liddell, Helen Lambie, Mr Adams, and Mary Barrowman had already been presented with three overcoats, light grey, brown tweed, and fawn waterproof, to have added a blue melton over-coat with velvet collar may have been considered too much for a jury's nerves And so Miss Brown stood down The Jury never heard of her existence On point of education and maturity of judgment this witness was more entitled to be heard than a young message girl—but that did not count. Miss Brown, had she gone into the box would have proved that Barrowman was totally wrong in the direction in which the presumable fugitive fled from the scene, and on the principle that an empty house is better than a bad tenant, the Crown apparently denied her the right to speak to the Jury, although they had brought her there for the purpose of doing so

If we include the Glasgow and Liverpool porters, clerks, etc., Dr Adams, Superintendent Douglas and the important witness McBrayne, the Crown ignored a round dozen of people speaking favourably of the prisoner or upsetting the line of proof they were to proceed upon against the prisoner It is a strange right this, fundamentally opposed to justice and to the public uses of the police and prosecution departments of our Criminal System, that what they get in the way of evidence becomes their absolute property and may be used against the prisoner or turned down, suppressed and silenced if it does not suit their case

DISAGREEMENTS IN EVIDENCE

Throughout the various stages of the preparation of the case as we have endeavoured to depict it, one thing seems to have become clear a steady, directing intelligence in the selection or evidence working, uniformly, towards the end of contriving to make the actions of the prisoner before and after the crime take on a guilty look Now we intend to show another phase of the prosecution making for the same end This consisted in a departure sometimes very slight but telling always, in the evidence of the witnesses when they came to appear in Court from the original statements made by them to the police. This Slater case is unique in respect of the public getting an insight into the methods of preparing for a murder trial because from the revelations by Trench we have obtained possession of the original statements of the witnesses, and these are always kept inviolably secret. There were also the New York proceedings—making three occasions for testing the credibility, etc, of the particular witnesses. So far as the witnesses are concerned we cast no imputations whatever upon their honour or integrity.) We are dealing always with the effects upon the prisoner's case of these errors, deviations, or departures innocently made by them, call these what you may. For the purpose of exhibiting this inner aspect of the case we place in juxtaposition the first statements of certain of the witnesses and their evidence as finally presented to the Jury.

Name of Witness	First Statements	Evidence at Trial
Detective Gordon	Speaking of Slater's maid Schmalz "She told me she *did not know* where he had gone, but thought London"	The maid told me that Slater had left the night before for London
John Forsyth Clerk in Cunard Coy's office, Liverpool	"He said he had just come from Glasgow and was staying at the North Western Hotel"	He said he would not take the room as it had been offered through an Agent in Glasgow and kind of turned to withdraw that"

Name of Witness	First Statement	Evidence at Trial
John Forsyth (cont.) This witness was awarded £40 by the Fiscal for his supposed assistance in effecting the arrest		Under cross examination — and when you say he apparently wanted to withdraw that do you mean that he did not want to pursue that or seemed to regret having said it?' Well, it seemed to me he was rather sorry he had made the remark. [There was a letter in Court from Cook's Agents to the Cunard Co. Liverpool, informing them that Oscar Slater, Glasgow, would call and book berths.] Not a word about Slater's staying in the North-Western Hotel, Liverpool
	(Not a word about 'Sorry he made the remark etc.')	
Helen Lambie	A grey Coat	A fawn waterproof coat
	At New York— knew him by his walk	'Knew him by his face.'
	'Like the man	'He is the man
(Re Lambie) Detective Gordon	She told me she would not be able to identify the man	Not a word
Detective Pyper	She told me she did not think she would be able to identify the man	Not a word
Barrowman	Went to Brother's shop learned of murder 8 15 p m	Went to Band of Hope meeting, learned of murder 10 p m
This witness was awarded £100 for her assistance in effecting the arrest of Slater	'Tall and thin'	'Tall and square-shouldered *
	"He passed close to me'	He knocked into me This repeated seven times

*At the New York proceedings the solicitor for Slater asked the Commissioner there to note that Barrowman's first description 'Tall and thin' was disconform to Slater's appearance

Name of Witness	Prior Statement	Evidence at Trial
Barrowman (cont.)	something like the man, then very like	'That is the man.'
	Asked at New York if she had seen photographs of Slater and identified them, answered "yes"	Detective Pyper denied that she had identified the photographs at New York. Pyper was present and said she could not identify
Mrs. Barrowman	Said that "Mary" told her she had been to Band of Hope meeting	Two detectives who were present said that Mary told them she had gone to her brother's shop. No mention of Band of Hope meeting by the Officers
Superintendent Ord	Declared to the Jury the prisoner had covered up his tracks as far as possible	Compare with full statement made to Commissioner at 1914 Inquiry
	Compare this statement with Appendix 4. McLean reported Slater for exhibiting the pawn-ticket for diamond brooch	Stated that Allan McLean reported Slater to the police because of his resemblance to the description,' furnished by Mary Barrowman and published in the press, of the wanted man

ERRORS OF THE LORD ADVOCATE AND JUDGE

Considering the long distance we have travelled through a jungle of confusions and blunders, one would expect when one arrives at the trial in the highest criminal Tribunal in Scotland there should at last be found only the firm, sure ground of fact undisturbed by the admission of error. The public expects that the great trained legal minds, entrusted with the prosecution or presidence over the proceedings would in their handling of the case, display absolute immunity from traces of added error   Unfortunately, that was not so in this Slater case   The Lord Advocate, who prosecuted, added very seriously to the mistakes, all more or less damaging to the prisoner, while, with all deference to his memory, Lord Guthrie made several slips, one of which had the effect of destroying the alibi that had been set up on behalf of the prisoner   As regards the address of the Lord Advocate a question was raised by Sir Edward Marshall Hall in the House of Commons, in which reference was made to the " inaccurate statement of facts " which it contained   These were unfortunately many   To these we propose to refer briefly   The address in its general tenor, we consider to have offended that excellent maxim of Immanuel Kant, that eloquence should not be employed by the prosecution , its weight and influence should be reserved for the defence   The Lord Advocate overstrained matters when he declared that the prisoner had beforehand familiarised himself with the movements and habits of the occupants of the house of the victim " with a careful, prolonged and steady watching with a skilled eye ", and to which he added that the moment of entrance chosen by the assailant was

" the supreme opportunity "—a view irreconcilable with the circumstances of the ten minutes'
absence of the maid. That was a mistake in
which Lord Guthrie also partially joined The
Lord Advocate declared that the murderer
did not know the arrangements of the house—
this to explain away the small amount of jewellery
abstracted ; whereas the assailant went through
the box with the private papers and, moreover,
declined to remove jewellery visible at his very
hand He also advised the Jury, upon which
there wasn't a particle of evidence, and which
he could not, and did not do, " that in the sequel
he would show how that the prisoner came to
know that the victim was possessed of jewels "
There was no evidence on the point before the
Court. We earlier published the contents of an
official document, the terms of which made it
clear that the police had only guessed a probable
source of information as to possession of jewels.
He likewise informed the Jury that Slater's name
and his full description appeared in the Glasgow
evening papers on the afternoon of 25th December, and that this was the cause of the prisoner's
precipitate flight from Glasgow, and he
insinuated that Slater would have read the
papers and then hastened on with his packing
Apart from the absence of Slater's name, which
did not appear in any newspaper till he was at

mid-Atlantic, the so-called published description disagreed in every vital detail with Slater, the age was far wrong, he was described as "tall and thin," while Slater officially on the police books was 5 ft 8 ins, stout and square shoulders (he weighed over 13 stones)) He stated also that Slater had come to the Sloper Club, late on the night of the murder "gasping and panting for money," while Slater that day had drawn £30 from Liddell the pawnbroker. He stated that Mr Adams had declared Slater to have been " the man " whom he observed to leave the victim's house Mr. Adams, in evidence, had declared " I pointed out Slater, but I did not say he was the man " He stated that Cook's, the Glasgow agents for the Cunard Company, Liverpool, was " the last place in the world " Slater could return to if he wished to consult his own safety There was actually tabled in the Court when that statement was made the original letter by Messrs Cook to the Cunard Company in Liverpool, which stated that Oscar Slater would probably call next day and book berths for New York   That letter should have warned Forsyth, the witness, to be on the look-out for Slater at the Cunard Company's office

It is necessary here to interpolate that the Lord Advocate was himself a very much misinformed man   The Lord Advocate could never have made the reference he did to Slater's flight or his failure to have his house and furniture taken over in Glasgow (both entirely wrong) if the information known to the local authorities had been passed to him But, again, as there was no evidence before the Court to directly support these observations, the Lord Advocate was in grave error in theorising merely upon what the prisoner had done

This last observation applies likewise to the terms of the charge to the Jury by Lord Guthrie His Lordship, we submit, theorised too much, and travelled far from the facts before the Court There was a straining of matters when he declared to the Jury " the man's life has been not only a lie for years but is so to-day " Slater had never been convicted of any charge, and there is in existence a secret police document which declared that they could not have proved the charge suggested against Slater His Lordship also travelled far beyond the facts before the Court when he said " I never knew a case like the present, either in my own experience or from reading What is his name ? He knows, and probably Antoine knows, but that the Crown, with all its means of investigation, has failed to find out " Then, again, " we do not know where he was born , who his parents are, etc " ?*) In all this his Lordship was grievously in error / No evidence was led to show 'that the police had investigated the antecedents of the prisoner, while the witness for defence, Hugh Cameron, disclosed that on the night before Slater left Glasgow, he, the witness, had assisted Slater to procure a £5 Bank of England note which had been sent off by registered letter from Hope Street branch, addressed to Slater's father in Germany) His Lordship, if he intended to comment upon Slater's want of information as to birth, parentage, etc , should have taken from that witness what the name and address in Germany were. If we mistake not, the receipt for the registered letter was available in Court All this was most damaging to the prisoner and his Lordship was not warranted from the facts before the Court in saying so to the Jury Slater's real name was " Leschzner ", and he had dropped it because it was in English unpronounceable We also consider that his Lordship made a most serious slip in his reference to the absurd discrepancies in the descriptions put forward by the witnesses to identification His statement to the Jury was ("A difference of dress amounts

---

*Immediately on the conclusion of the trial an interview with Slater's mother residing in Silesia was published by a Glasgow newspaper , while a sister in Germany corresponds to this day with the prisoner at Peterhead Convict Establishment

to nothing because the way in which the prisoner
is dressed now is not necessarily the way he was
dressed at the time " That observation was very
wide of the remark in its application to the
testimony of the chief witnesses to identification
Lambie, Adams Barrowman Liddell saw him
within a period certified by themselves, restricted
to fifteen minutes   and all gave different
description of garments   His Lordship's reference was, therefore, not in the least apropos
the circumstances   That statement by Lord
Guthrie, if the Jury gave it due heed, virtually
made good for the prosecution the hopeless
identification by these four contradictory eye-
witnesses on the vital point of clothing   In the
Starchfield murder case, where there were far
less discrepancy in the contradictory descriptions,
the Prosecution, with the concurrence of the
Judge, abandoned the case

His Lordship also might have more fully com-
mented upon the grievous deviations by the
witness Lambie in her several standpoints
First, the grey coat, next the lawn waterproof to
coincide with Barrowman, and then that
grotesque blunder of declaring that a fawn coat
held up to her in Court was the very coat the
prisoner had four months before worn   Further,
there were her wobblings from walk to face, etc
Rejection in toto of her evidence is what should

have followed. It was likewise most regrettable that to the many grave errors committed in the submission of the case against this tortured man, his Lordship should have added still another that was most serious. This was a blunder which practically destroyed the prisoner's alibi—all the more regrettable when there has been discovered the suppressed evidence of the witness McBrayne, which completed a perfect alibi. His Lordship explained to the Jury that as regards the defence put up by the prisoner that he dined in his own house on the night in question, there was really nothing incompatible with it and the case for the prosecution. Slater, he explained, lived only a few streets off, and, as the murder was committed at 7 p.m., there was nothing to hinder him running from the house of the victim and being home for dinner, say, by 7 30 p m. In this his Lordship made the most hurtful omission that the Crown case was that Slater went down the subway steps, Kelvinside, at 7 30 p m, and rushed to the suburbs to hide and then to return home at a very much later hour. The Crown case was that Slater did not dine in his own house on the night of the murder at any hour whatsoever. The conclusion one is apt to come to after consideration of these many serious errors is one of wonder that there were even found six men in the jury box who gave

Slater the benefit of the doubt, and voted
" Not Proven " Not a single element of the case
but had error thrown into the scale against
the prisoner, apart altogether from the secret
manipulation of witnesses and documents by
suppression, etc., which we have shown to have
taken place before the Court proceedings began
We conclude with the observation that we do
not find in the case a single incident or circumstance in which the prisoner's position was justly
presented to the Court, and despite all this
Slater, after twenty years, is still held in prison
as the properly, truly, and justly convicted
murderer of Miss Gilchrist

And it is still more shocking to the conscience
and disturbing to one's confidence in the fairness
of the British criminal system to find that the
prisoner is denied every right of redress against
the many palpable and undesirable wrongs done
to him in bringing about his conviction   Not
less so that the highest officials, entrusted with
the administration of justice are content to
permit the Criminal Courts to stand charged
with the serious offences against their procedure
which have been repeatedly made by eminent
authorities and the Press in connection with this
notorious case, and which are here repeated with
fuller disclosure and completed proof of miscarriage of justice

LIEUTENANT TRENCH'S THEORY OF THE MURDER

The writer deems it not inappropriate to introduce as an interesting addendum, the solution to the mystery which was propounded by that able officer Trench, whose belief in the innocence of Slater and the falsity and blundering of the Crown prosecution, so moved his conscience as to reveal the secret documents and witnesses and led him to sacrifice 'place, pension and prestige " From the circumstances of the crime, as investigated by himself and his study of the statements by brother officers, Trench, before his death, furnished to the writer the following reconstructed story of the occurrence of the tragedy, as he believed it to have actually happened

The man who called at the house when the servant had gone out for the newspaper was on intimate terms of relationship with the victim. There was between them, however, a feud of some bitter sort (A relative declared before the 1914 Commissioner that the deceased was not on friendly terms with certain people) His object in coming to the house was to force her to yield up some document which she possessed and in which he was interested He came without intention to murder, and he brought with him no weapon His visit was to her unexpected

He rang the bell and was admitted by Miss Gilchrist. Together they proceeded on her invitation to the fireplace in the dining-room where her seat was. As they did so, the old lady who could be at times snappy and querulous, turned upon him and sneeringly asked "What brings *you* here?"—or similar biting remark. The sting of this taunt irritated and provoked the visitor, containing as it did a reminder of past unpleasantness. The visitor was in no gracious mood himself, and in a sudden access of rage he struck her a swinging blow which sent her reeling to the floor. In the act of falling, her head came in violent contact with the coal box, the bone of the skull was penetrated on the side of the head (The coal-box showed signs afterwards of blood, and was itself broken and displaced from its earlier position). The result of the contact was attended with serious results obvious to him. He saw she had been badly stunned and was making no signs to rise. He stooped down, quickly examined her, and judged there was a grave danger of fatal consequences, but not just at once. He was aware that if she survived beyond ten minutes, which seemed a certainty, and the maid were to reappear his name would be disclosed, and in the event of death ensuing, he would be accused of murder. At that moment of grave uncertainty and

danger for him flight was impossible   To do so
would be the worst of all possible lines of action.
He thereupon decided to take the awful step of
killing her outright and silencing her lips which
would give him some chance of an outlet from
his dreadful predicament   Trench declared that
Dr Adams was correct in the use of the chair
as the weapon   Driven to despair, he seized a
chair and hacked at the prostrate woman in his
haste to extinguish life and get away before
Lambie reappeared on the scene   When the bell
rang, he knew that someone else had come to the
door, Lambie having the keys, and so he went on,
not desisting until satisfied she was far beyond
the possibility of utterance   Even then he still
delayed exit   There was a paper in the box of
which he wanted possession   If it were to
remain, probably its contents would throw
suspicion upon him   So he went into the bedroom where he knew she kept the documents,
seized and broke open the box, and removed the
paper he desired   He then slipped out unchal-
lenged—because the servant knew him and his
presence allayed rather than excited her suspicion   As regards the theft of the brooch—
in this story Trench had no faith.   The article,
he said, was never proved to have existed . it
was only a statement from Lambie, whose mind,

*Trench: no-brooch theory
 Hunt: lambie lost the brooch...

as Lord Guthrie said at the trial, was " unreflec-
tive " and not to be too seriously taken. In
the alternative case, it was only a " blind," and
its removal, if that happened, had nothing to do
with his objects in visiting the house

Trench offered no solution to the problem
what would have happened to the servant-maid,
supposing Adams had not appeared on the scene ?
It was beyond deduction Lord Guthrie
declared at the trial two murders was the possible
outcome, but this assumed murder as the motive
of the visit In that Trench did not at all
believe The crime was really an accident—
unforeseen, uncontemplated It arose from the
feud, the jibe from the old lady, the answer of
that with a blow and the accident of the fall
on the coal-box Trench also considered the
proper clue was the finding of bloodstains on the
trousers worn by the assailant at that part above
the foot which rested on the chest of the deceased
and was below the seat of the chair, which was the
shielding agent for the upper part of the garments
and hands against the ejected blood spurts.

It might be added that on his perusal of the
evidence at the trial Sir Herbert Stephen con-
gratulated this officer upon the honesty and
straightforwardness of his statements. Trench
answered the questions straightforwardly which,
under cross-examination, showed the unsatis-

factory character of the identification proceedings against Slater.

We conclude with one more observation. The tragedy of Miss Gilchrist's death was three-fold in character. There was first, the deprivation of the victim's life under circumstances of the most shocking callousness and brutality, second, the conviction by the most patent and repeated blunderings by the police of an innocent man, and third, the persecution and martyrdom of the capable officer who attempted to remedy the wrong done to the prisoner. It is not out of place here to indicate as a further tragic sequel that both Lieutenant Trench and the Glasgow solicitor, who supported the officer in his fight for justice, were subsequently arrested on a trumpery charge so scandalously out of place the Judge tore it to tatters and virtually called for an explanation of it, while the Jury, without the trouble to leave the box, unanimously dismissed it " Not Guilty."

APPENDIX
No 1

NOTE.—The prisoner's story, as furnished to his law agent while in Duke Street Prison, Glasgow, in preparation for the trial at Edinburgh. This statement was taken by the late Mr Ewing Speirs, of Messrs Shaughnessy & Co, and was passed to the writer, authenticated by the firm, in its original form. Slater intended to give his own statement to the Jury, but after four days' strenuous and painful ordeal, his Counsel, having regard to his broken English, deemed it prudent not to put his client in the box The original statement of the prisoner as so taken is now presented with slight annotations to make clear the significance of the various points

"I am thirty-seven years of age I am a Jew I was born in Germany. I left that country because I did not wish to serve in the Army When I came to this country I acted as a bookmaker's clerk I stayed in Glasgow and Edinburgh. I was married seven years ago in Glasgow to May Curtis Our marriage was unfortunate. I met Antoine about five years ago in London I was residing at the time in Russell Square. About eighteen months later

we left for Brussels, where we stayed together
for about three weeks We visited New York
and stayed there for about a year Paris was our
next place of residence, two months being spent
there It was London next, spending several
months in that City

"We came to Glasgow about the beginning of
November last or the end of October I stayed
for some days in the Central Station Hotel, and
thereafter for some time at 138 Renfrew Street,
Glasgow About the middle of November I
rented a flat at 69 St George's Road I had it
furnished on the instalment system I paid
them £16 Miss Antoine, who is a French-
woman, was with me there, and we had a servant-
maid named Catherine Schmalz I frequented
the M O S C Club in India Street I have also
been in the Motor Club next door For some
time prior to 25th December, 1908, I had formed
the ambition to go back to America, as I thought I
would make more money there I had received
a letter from a friend called John De Voto in San
Francisco asking me to come out I showed
this letter to my friends, Rattman and Cameron,
and I frequently stated my intention of going
to America with my friends With this view I was
in negotiation with a Mr Aumann (a witness at the
trial) to try to get him to take over my furnished
flat I understand that his wife did not agree

with this idea and negotiations fell through   I
thereafter wrote to a friend of mine in London
called Freedman asking him to take over my
flat, and I made up my mind to leave Glasgow
immediately his wife came."

"Mrs. Freedman and her sister, Elsie Hoppe,
arrived at my flat on Friday, 25th December,
1908, and I gave her the keys of the house. She
made no payment to me but this was to be sent
on."

NOTE —This evidence of Slater's, afterwards
admitted by the police to be correct, destroyed
the whole story laid to his charge at the trial by
Superintendent Ord and the Lord Advocate
that it was the publication of his name and
description (that also totally wrong) which sent
Slater flying out of Glasgow after the murder.
Ord told the 1914 Commissioner that when
Freedman called, she found Slater " packing
up " What else was he to have done since he
had brought the people from London who were
to take over his flat, and had actually installed
them ?

" Miss Antoine and I left Glasgow with the
9 5 p.m. train from the Central Station.   I had
that evening taken two tickets for Liverpool—
one for myself and one for Antoine. My luggage
was labelled for Liverpool at the station.   I did

not change trains The carriage that I travelled in went right through to Liverpool."

NOTE.—This refers to a statement in the early newspaper reports, prompted by the police, that Slater took London tickets but broke his journey and went on to Liverpool We also showed that in this statement Slater was challenged by railway officials as being in error as to the through-carriage to Liverpool, and his persistence in this led them at length to remember that it was Christmas night and that a special through-carriage had been added.

"My luggage consisted of nine boxes and a parcel. My luggage was weighed at the station, and I had to pay excess rate amounting to £1 2s. 6d I asked for Liverpool tickets No one challenged the tickets."

NOTE.—The police attempted to make out at the trial that he took tickets for London. The information from Liverpool was there were "only two tickets" handed up there, while, if he had occupied the through Liverpool carriage the guard or inspector checking the tickets would have instructed him to leave the carriage and these officials would have been produced as witnesses against him

"We sailed by the *Lusitania* for New York next day, having previously put up at the North Western Hotel, Liverpool We took the name of Mr and Mrs. Otto Sando from the hotel   I wrote a letter to Max Rattman (produced at the trial)   I took the name of Otto Sando because my luggage was labelled 'O S', and I did not wish to travel under the name Oscar Slater, as I did not wish my wife to have trace of me   Our servant, Catherine Schmalz, saw us off in the train from the Central Station and it was arranged that she should remain with the Freedmans in our Glasgow flat for a day or so

"I know nothing about the murder of Miss Gilchrist   I never heard of her or her servant before the murder, and when the police stopped me at New York that was the first intimation that I ever had   I was suspected   The police found a pawn-ticket in my pocket for a gold brooch set with three rows of diamonds   This brooch belonged to Miss Antoine   I had pawned it with Mr Liddell, pawnbroker, Sauchiehall Street, about the middle of November, 1908   During the week on which I left Glasgow, I endeavoured to sell this ticket to various people but did not succeed   I remember being in Galls' Public House in the afternoon of Monday, 21st December (day of tragedy), where I met Rattman and Aumann   I tried to sell the pawn-ticket then   I went alone also that afternoon to Miller's public-house in Cambridge Street, to try to sell the ticket. I remember that evening later I was with Rattman and Aumann in Johnstone's billiard room, and I remember shortly after 6 p m sending a telegram from Central Station Telegraph Office to Dent, London, for my watch, which was under repair   If I said in some of my telegrams to him that I was going to the Continent this was simply to hurry him up

"My recollection is that I was in Miller's public-house that evening shortly before seven o'clock and went straight home for dinner, arriving there at seven o'clock [the moment of the tragedy], but I may be wrong in this [it is to be remembered Slater was here speaking at a date two months after events] and may have come from Johnstone's billiard rooms, leaving it about 6 30 p m and arriving home at 7 o'clock   After dinner I may have left my house between seven and eight o'clock   I cannot remember definitely where I spent the remainder of the evening "

NOTE —It is to be recollected that the witness McBrayne, unheard at the trial, found Slater at the foot of his stairway at 8 15 p m

" I am aware that the witness Henderson has said that on the night of the murder about a quarter to ten I called at his Club, the Motor Club, and asked for the loan of money   I am almost sure I did not do so that night   As a matter of fact I had that very day obtained from

Mr Liddell, pawnbroker, a further allowance of £30 on the brooch   I had no bills to pay   I remember borrowing some money from Beveridge and I am quite sure that it was the same night that I borrowed the money from Beveridge that I asked Henderson for the money   I understand Beveridge states that I borrowed from him on the Saturday night previous to the night of the murder   This is likely to be right.   I did not go back immediately to the M.O.S.C Club after talking to Henderson.   I cannot remember anything more as to how I spent the Monday evening. I had no notice until I reached America that I would ever be called upon to explain, and to me that night is just like any other night."

NOTE —Slater did not ascertain the date of the murder until some time after his arrest at New York.   It would probably be almost a month before he was asked to say where he had been on the night of the tragedy.

"I may say that I ordered Christmas cards from More, Sauchiehall Street, with my name, Oscar Slater, on them, on the 19th December [this, two days before the murder : an act which makes ridiculous the police story of prior watching of Miss Gilchrist's house and flight so soon as the crime was over].

"During the rest of the week after the Monday I went about just as usual.   I frequented my

usual billiard rooms, the Crown billiard rooms
and Johnstone's billiard rooms   I called at my
usual barbers, Charing Cross, and was shaved
In this connection I may explain that I had a
short black moustache   When I left Glasgow
I had been letting it grow for about two weeks
I spent Thursday afternoon with my friend,
Cameron, about the city   I posted a Bank of
England £5 note to my people in Germany that
afternoon in a registered envelope at Hope
Street Post Office

"Regarding the hammer found in my box
I purchased it from Messrs Hepburn & Marshall,
Charing Cross I wanted a hammer to fix things
up when I took possession of my flat, but instead
of buying a hammer alone, I saw a card with
hammers and other tools on it and I bought the
lot for 2s 6d. I took it with us to America as
part of my belongings   I think it was in a box
in the hold during the voyage

"I did not cut any holes in my waterproof
These may have been mud-stains on the waterproof as it got frequently splashed with mud
I know of no other stains" (NOTE —The
Crown cut the holes to examine some stains on
the coat for blood   None found.) "The hammer was never washed so far as I am aware

"It is not true that on the night of the murder
I rushed through Kelvinbridge Subway or that I

ran along West Princes Street   I was in neither
of those places that night "

NOTE.—McBrayne corroborated, but he was
ignored

" I never loitered about West Princes Street.
I never inquired at any house there for anybody
called Anderson   I never stood in that street
during the day about one o'clock   I usually had
lunch at 1 p m in my house

" It is not the case that on the Sunday evening
before the murder I was loitering about on the
street   I was in the house on the whole of that
Sunday and dined on that evening with Antoine
and a man named Reid, who did not leave the
house till about 10 o'clock "

[This is in denial of a statement by two witnesses, Bryson and Grant, who told the Jury
they saw a man like Slater in West Princes Street
Their identification was far from satisfactory
One said that at a distance of thirteen yards he
knew him by his " back " The man spoken of
as Reid corroborated Slater at the trial that he
had dined with the prisoner at his house]

" I am informed that Rattman says that a few
nights after the murder he referred to it, and that
I had said I had not heard of it.   This must be a
mistake   I remember we were standing near my
house about midnight on one occasion   and
what I certainly meant was that I had not known

that the scene of the murder was so near at hand. We then went to have a look at the street where it took place

' The witnesses who tried to identify me (Lambie and Barrowman) in America in the American Court, were standing at the end of a corridor, and I was brought along the corridor between a marshall, 6 ft 2 ins in height, and another official One of these officials had on a badge These witnesses could not help knowing that I was in charge of these men "

[Some other minor items not included]

No 2 *— search warrant application*

Humbly showeth.

That the Petitioner has charged Oscar Slater, alias Otto Sando, alias Anderson, sometimes of 69 St George's Road. Glasgow, *with the crime of murder of Miss Marion Gilchrist,* in her house at 15 Queen's Terrace, West Princes Street, Glasgow, on 21st December, 1908

That it appears that said Oscar Slater, alias Otto Sando, alias Anderson, was on said date, and for some time before and some time thereafter in a house at 69 St George's Road, aforesaid, taken by him in name of " A Anderson," and *that he has since absconded*

That it seems necessary that a search be made of the house, clothing, papers and repositories therein, and the petitioner therefore craves warrant to officers of law to search the said house where the said Oscar Slater, alias Otto Sando, alias Anderson, then resided, and all papers, clothing and repositories therein.

May it therefore please your Lordship to grant warrant to search for and secure for the purpose of precognition all articles, papers, clothing or documents found 'therein, importing guilt or participation in the crime foresaid

According to Justice,

(Sgd) James N. Hart, P.F

Glasgow, 2nd January, 1909

The Sheriff Substitute grants warrant as craved

(Sgd.) A. T. Glegg.

NOTE —This document shows that the house vacated by Slater was searched for all articles " importing guilt " None was found, which converts the document into another argument in favour of the prisoner's innocence.

No 3

MINNIE HEPBURN or HAMILTON

[Statement of evidence given to Slater's agent in May, 1909, and re-confirmed at date of publication]

" I am twenty-nine years of age. Up to a short time ago I had a restaurant at 415 Argyle Street. At that time I was staying at my present address.

"I have a friend named Mrs Roger, who stays in Argyle Street, Maryhill, and I am in the habit of visiting her She is a great friend of mine.

"I remember the evening of 21st December, 1908, I had been up at Mrs Roger's that evening I had taken the car there, but, as I am fond of walking, I walked back to my restaurant in Argyle Street.

"I left Mrs. Roger's house some time after six o'clock, not later than 6 30 anyway. I cannot remember what street I took after leaving New City Road, but after leaving Great Western Road, I went through Melrose Street, Queen's Terrace and into West Princes Street

"So soon as I got into West Princes Street I crossed to the opposite side of the road (I was proceeding down West Princes Street when a man came running down so quickly that he knocked up against me and knocked me down I was knocked right off the pavement I saw him as he was coming down the steps He was a man of about medium height, slimly built, with a Donegal hat on and a light waterproof, brown leggings and brown boots He had a fair moustache, and it was pretty long at the points It was a heavy moustache)

"The waterproof had a wide sack back and came down to the top of his leggings. So far as I could see there was no split in the back of the waterproof

" So far as I could see the man had a thin face. The Donegal hat was well pulled down over his eyes   He had both hands in his pockets

" I was suprised at the time, as the man did not offer to apologise to me nor help me up, but ran on at full speed towards St George's Road. I got up and looked after him as he ran away. I did not see anybody else in the street at the time.

" I arrived at my shop in Argyle Street about a quarter to eight   I think the incident I refer to would happen about 7 15 p m

" I thought nothing more of it at the time, nor did I connect this man in any way with the murder until the day of Miss Gilchrist's funeral I think on that day there was a photo of Miss Gilchrist's house in the newspaper. Whenever I saw the photo of the house I remarked to the servant in the house that it was there I was knocked down by the man   I had not mentioned to anyone that I had been knocked down in West Princes Street

" When I saw the photo of the house and with what I read in the newspaper about when the murder took place, I at once thought that this man might have had something to do with it

" I recognised the house at once I have been in West Princes Street several times since, and I have recognised Miss Gilchrist's close as the place out of which the man came. I did not see any other person in the street at the time

" I did not know about the murder until next morning I also mentioned the incident to my husband when I saw the photograph of Miss Gilchrist's house

" When Slater was brought from America I wanted to go to the Shaughnessy's office and tell my story, but my husband did not want me to be mixed up with it and persuaded me not to go

" I have not told my husband about coming here to-day I happened to be up the same stair on other business, and I thought I would come in and tell what I had seen

" I have seen a photo of Slater in the newspaper and he is certainly not the man I saw running away that night "

No 4

[How the mistaken brooch clue disappeared from the case and a new originating clue was substituted to explain the arrest]

The following extract from a well-informed article in the " Empire News " draws attention to one point of the case which is of supreme importance, namely, the strange way in which when the original brooch clue broke down utterly, the cause of arrest was suddenly shifted on to quite another matter, and the Jury was so handled that it quite lost sight of the fact that the second reason had been substituted for the first —

"It is one of the new points against the police (and this is absolutely fresh to it) that the Jury was entirely misled at the trial as to the nature of the originating cause of the arrest of Slater, and that the Crown presented to the Court an absolutely new case, one that did not exist in reality, and was inconsistent to the known facts concerning his arrest

"This was achieved in the following manner before the Court As little as possible, apparently, was said about the brooch clue It only came out at the trial, furtively, and without clear and distinct reference to it having been the originating cause of Slater's arrest

"On the other hand, Superintendent Ord, as chief of the police, stated to the Jury that one Allan McLean reported to him that he had observed in the newspapers a description of the murderer, as provided by an eye-witness who had seen the culprit run along the street, and that he thought this description agreed with the man whom he knew, Slater

" Founding upon that statement, the Lord Advocate told the Jury that the description furnished by that eye-witness, Barrowman, had been so accurate it had enabled the police to trace the prisoner.

TWO DIFFERENT STORIES

" McLean said to the police —

" ' I noticed that after the murder of Miss Gilchrist on 21st December he (Slater) did not return to the club, and on hearing that he had been offering a pawn-ticket for a valuable diamond brooch, which was alleged to have been pledged for £50 on the day of the murder, I, on Friday, 25th December, went to the detective department, Central Police Office, and reported the matter.'

" Nothing there about the resemblance to a description he had read in the papers between it and Slater

" Before the 1914 Commissioner, who afterwards inquired into the case, here is what McLean said on the question of what made him report Slater to the police :—

" ' It was not so much his absence from the club that directed my suspicion towards him *as his offering the pawn-ticket for sale* '

' Here is what Ord said to the Jury —

"'About 6·10 p m on 25th December the witness Allan McLean called at the Central Police Office He gave me information where a man of the description (published that day in the paper) was to be found *He said that in consequence of the description having appeared in the newspapers, he had called to give me information about the man*'

"The Jury got a new story altogether They believed that Slater was arrested because in appearance he was like the man who ran out of the house of the victim The truth was he was arrested because he had a pawn-ticket for a diamond brooch, which was his own property "

MADE AND PRINTED IN GREAT BRITAIN
BY
JOSEPH WONES, WEST BROMWICH

MEMORIES and ADVENTURES

BY

ARTHUR CONAN DOYLE

7|6

Memories of Medical Life. Memories of Sport. Memories of Literature. Memories of Psychic Experience. Adventures in the Arctic and the Tropics. Adventures in Three Wars. Account of the Edalji Case. Account of the Oscar Slater Case. Records of a Busy and Varied Life.

PSYCHIC PRESS, 2, Victoria Street, S.W.

CPSIA information can be obtained at www.ICGtesting.com
Printed in the USA
BVOW020948130313

315455BV00003B/43/P